HISTORY & GEOGRAPHY 10
Renaissance and Reformation

LIFEPAC Test is located in the center of the booklet. Please remove before starting the unit.

Author:
Helen Robertson Prewitt, M.A.Ed.

Editor-in-Chief:
Richard W. Wheeler, M.A.Ed.

Editor:
J. Douglas Williamson

Consulting Editor:
Howard Stitt, Th.M., Ed.D.

Revision Editor:
Alan Christopherson, M.S.

MEDIA CREDITS:
Page 10: © Sodacan; **14:** © Sodacan; **18:** © Heralder; **26:** © Freedoo, iStock, Thinkstock
32: © JackJelly, iStock, Thinkstock; **36:** © GeorgiosArt, iStock, Thinkstock; **39:** © Georgios Kollidas, iStock, Thinkstock; **46:** © Photos.com, Thinkstock; **51:** Dorling Kindersley, Thinkstock.

804 N. 2nd Ave. E.
Rock Rapids, IA 51246-1759

Renaissance and Reformation

Introduction

The medieval systems of government, social structure, culture, science, and religion underwent significant changes within a span of only a few centuries. This contact with other cultures and civilizations led to increased exploration and trade and to the development of cities. A spirit of inquiry led scholars to study classic Greek and Roman literature. From a society organized around feudalism and the church, Western Europe evolved into a society composed of strong monarchies.

In this LIFEPAC®, you will trace this change through the transitional period known as the Renaissance. In the first section, you will be especially aware of changes in government, the arts, literature and thought, and science.

In the second section, you will study changes in religion. Catholicism had been a cohesive force in medieval Europe. During the Later Middle Ages, religious unrest developed into a movement known as the Protestant Reformation. This movement involved such men as John Wycliffe, Martin Luther, and John Calvin. The Reformation in England involved political, as well as religious changes and issues. You will learn more about the Protestant influences, as well as about reforms within the Catholic Church. All of these religious changes culminated in a series of religious wars which influenced most of Europe.

Objectives

Read these objectives. The objectives tell you what you will be able to do when you have successfully completed this LIFEPAC. When you have finished this LIFEPAC, you should be able to:

1. Trace the development of France, England, and Spain from feudal kingdoms to strong monarchies.
2. Trace the development of the five Italian states.
3. Identify and describe the developments made in the arts during the Renaissance.
4. Identify outstanding Renaissance writers and their work.
5. Identify major Renaissance scientists and explain their contributions to modern science.
6. Trace the European Protestant Reformation.
7. Trace the development of the Reformation in England.
8. Trace the Catholic reform movement.
9. Describe the impact of the religious wars upon Western Europe.

Survey the LIFEPAC. Ask yourself some questions about this study. Write your questions here.

1. THE RENAISSANCE

Toward the end of the Middle Ages, a movement known as the Renaissance arose. The Renaissance was a transitional period, bridging the gap from medieval to modern times. Various changes occurred during this period: changes in the governments of Western Europe, changes in the arts, changes in literature and thought, as well as changes in science.

In this section, you will learn how the feudal system gradually faded away, leaving the strong national powers of France, England, and Spain. Italy, although not a national power, had expanded her city-states into five powerful regions or states.

Architecture, rather than painting, was the main interest during the medieval period. Gothic, Romanesque, and Byzantine styles of architecture were combined into new forms. Some of the Renaissance artists you will learn more about include Michelangelo, Raphael, and Leonardo da Vinci. You may be surprised by the many accomplishments of these Renaissance men who became proficient in many fields, rather than specializing in just one area.

The Italian writers, Petrarch and Boccaccio, were actually transitional figures leading to the Italian Renaissance movement in literature. Their words influenced later Italians and other European writers. Literature flourished throughout Europe during this period.

Renaissance scientists ushered in a new approach to the study of science. Early in the thirteenth century, Roger Bacon had introduced experimentation as a scientific technique. Other outstanding scientists you will study include da Vinci, Copernicus, Galileo, Kepler, and Newton. Newton applied earlier knowledge in his discovery of laws of gravity.

Section Objectives

Review these objectives. When you have completed this section, you should be able to:

1. Trace the development of France, England, and Spain from feudal kingdoms to strong monarchies.
2. Trace the development of the five Italian states.
3. Identify and describe the developments made in the arts during the Renaissance.
4. Identify outstanding Renaissance writers and their works.
5. Identify major Renaissance scientists and explain their contributions to modern science.

Vocabulary

Study these words to enhance your learning success in this section.

bourgeoisie
humanities
poet laureate
Christian humanism
Moors
heliocentric
Neoplatonism

Note: *All vocabulary words in this LIFEPAC appear in* **boldface** *print the first time they are used. If you are not sure of the meaning when you are reading, study the definitions given.*

CHANGES IN GOVERNMENT

The medieval feudal system was gradually replaced by the development of commerce throughout Western Europe. Changes were occurring during this period of transition, especially in the areas of government, politics, and human rights. The people began to strive for personal freedom. Serfs were becoming freemen, and countries were becoming nations. Some of these changes were brought about through wars.

The concept of Roman law, which supported strong monarchs by granting them unlimited authority, was absorbed slowly into most European countries. The acceptance of this idea, in turn, denied many the rights of the nobility, thus weakening the feudal structure.

The feudal system had been an outgrowth of the search for military protection. By the late Middle Ages, new discoveries in weaponry had made it possible for kings to hire mercenaries (or professional soldiers) to fight for money, rather than for land and favors. Both the crossbow and the long bow made a knight's chain mail obsolete. Even armor had its drawbacks: Knights were clumsy and virtually helpless when unhorsed in battle. The development of gunpowder and cannons made it possible to storm even the most massive medieval castles. All of these developments replaced feudal war tactics.

The growth of trade, which was stimulated by the crusades and later exploration, encouraged the establishment of commercial towns. These centers of commerce supported a centralized government to protect their trade routes from roving bands of robbers. Out of this commercial development emerged a new class of people—the middle class. Since the medieval feudal and manorial systems included only the nobility and the peasants, they were not supported by this newer middle class. Members of the middle class began to find places for themselves in city government. Their loyalties were usually with the king rather than with the church, which disapproved of trade and banking.

France. The Treaty of Paris established between Louis IX and Henry III in 1259, temporarily formed the basis for foreign relations between France and England. Edward I, Henry's successor, also carried out the terms of the treaty. By this treaty, a large portion of French territory remained under the control of England, but France was dissatisfied with this arrangement. The English-held duchy of Aquitaine was also a trade center.

A disagreement between French and English sailors was used as an excuse by Philip VI to attempt his take-over of Aquitaine. At the same time, Philip VI and Edward III both claimed the French throne. This action resulted in war between the two countries, and an uneasy peace was achieved for a short period. Finally, Edward III decided to fight France in an effort to prevent the loss of English land in France and declared war in 1337. This intermittent fighting which lasted over a century was known as the Hundred Years' War. Although such issues as boundaries and feudal rights were involved, the underlying issue was the fact that the French could not accept English possession of French territory. Other factors leading to war included France's intervention against England in a dispute with Scotland and England's economic interest in Flanders, a French fief.

Flanders had been a center for weaving woolen cloth. Although France claimed Flemish allegiance through the Flemish count, the allegiance was not supported by the weavers. When the count tried to restrict trade with England, which supplied both the raw wool to Flanders and the market for the woolen products, the weavers overthrew him. Flanders then allied herself with England.

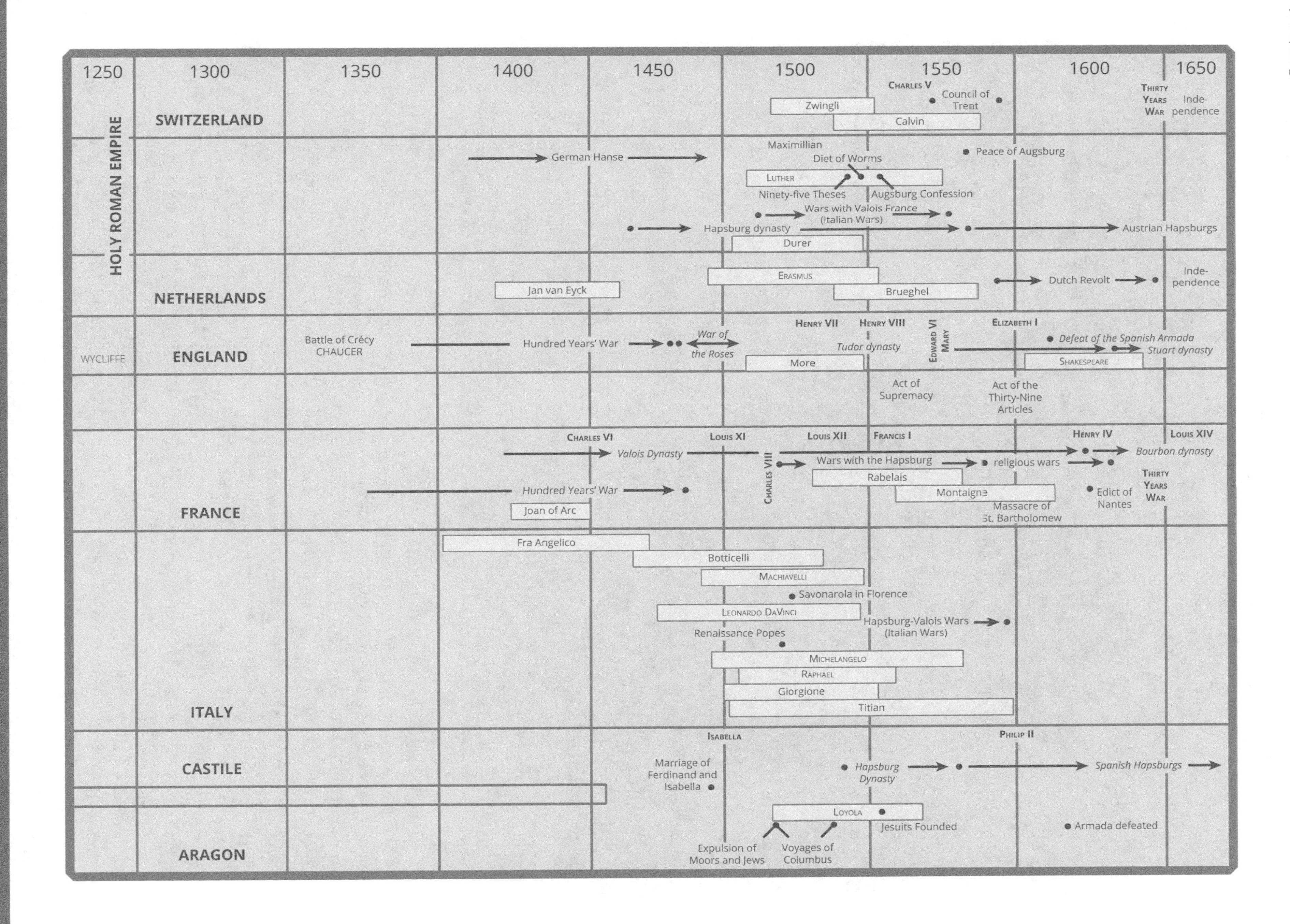
1250
1300
1350
1400
1450
1500
1550
1600
1650
HOLY ROMAN EMPIRE
SWITZERLAND
Charles V
Council of Trent
Zwingli
Calvin
Thirty Years War
Inde-pendence
German Hanse
Maximillian
Diet of Worms
Peace of Augsburg
Luther
Ninety-five Theses
Augsburg Confession
Wars with Valois France (Italian Wars)
Hapsburg dynasty
Austrian Hapsburgs
Durer
NETHERLANDS
Erasmus
Jan van Eyck
Brueghel
Dutch Revolt
Inde-pendence
WYCLIFFE
ENGLAND
Battle of Crécy
CHAUCER
Hundred Years' War
War of the Roses
Henry VII
Henry VIII
Tudor dynasty
Edward VI
Mary
Elizabeth I
Defeat of the Spanish Armada
Stuart dynasty
More
Shakespeare
Act of Supremacy
Act of the Thirty-Nine Articles
FRANCE
Charles VI
Valois Dynasty
Louis XI
Charles VIII
Louis XII
Francis I
Henry IV
Louis XIV
Bourbon dynasty
Wars with the Hapsburg
religious wars
Rabelais
Montaigne
Hundred Years' War
Joan of Arc
Massacre of St. Bartholomew
Edict of Nantes
Thirty Years War
ITALY
Fra Angelico
Botticelli
Machiavelli
Savonarola in Florence
Leonardo DaVinci
Hapsburg-Valois Wars (Italian Wars)
Renaissance Popes
Michelangelo
Raphael
Giorgione
Titian
CASTILE
Isabella
Philip II
Marriage of Ferdinand and Isabella
Hapsburg Dynasty
Spanish Hapsburgs
ARAGON
Loyola
Jesuits Founded
Armada defeated
Expulsion of Moors and Jews
Voyages of Columbus

The Battle of Crecy in 1346 resulted in the overwhelming defeat of the French forces. Calais was the next to be attacked. After a year long siege, the English finally overcame this strategically located town. England had gained control of the narrowest part of the English Channel. While they were attacking France, the English were unsuccessfully invaded by the Scots.

Other destructive raids were made on France. France suffered military devastation since all of the fighting had occurred in France. The Black Death had weakened the country as well. The Black Death, or bubonic plague, killed a large portion of the population.

All the pillaging and looting disgusted the French people who rebelled in protest against King John, the head of a weak government. Although these rebellions were put down, France was a defeated country. The Treaty of Calais in 1360 brought an apparent end to the war. Since the terms of the treaty restored to England all the French territories claimed by them, the French people were again provoked.

At the death of John in 1364, Charles V, sometimes called Charles "the Wise," ascended to the throne. His reign brought about the elimination of governmental corruption and the establishment of France as a strong nation.

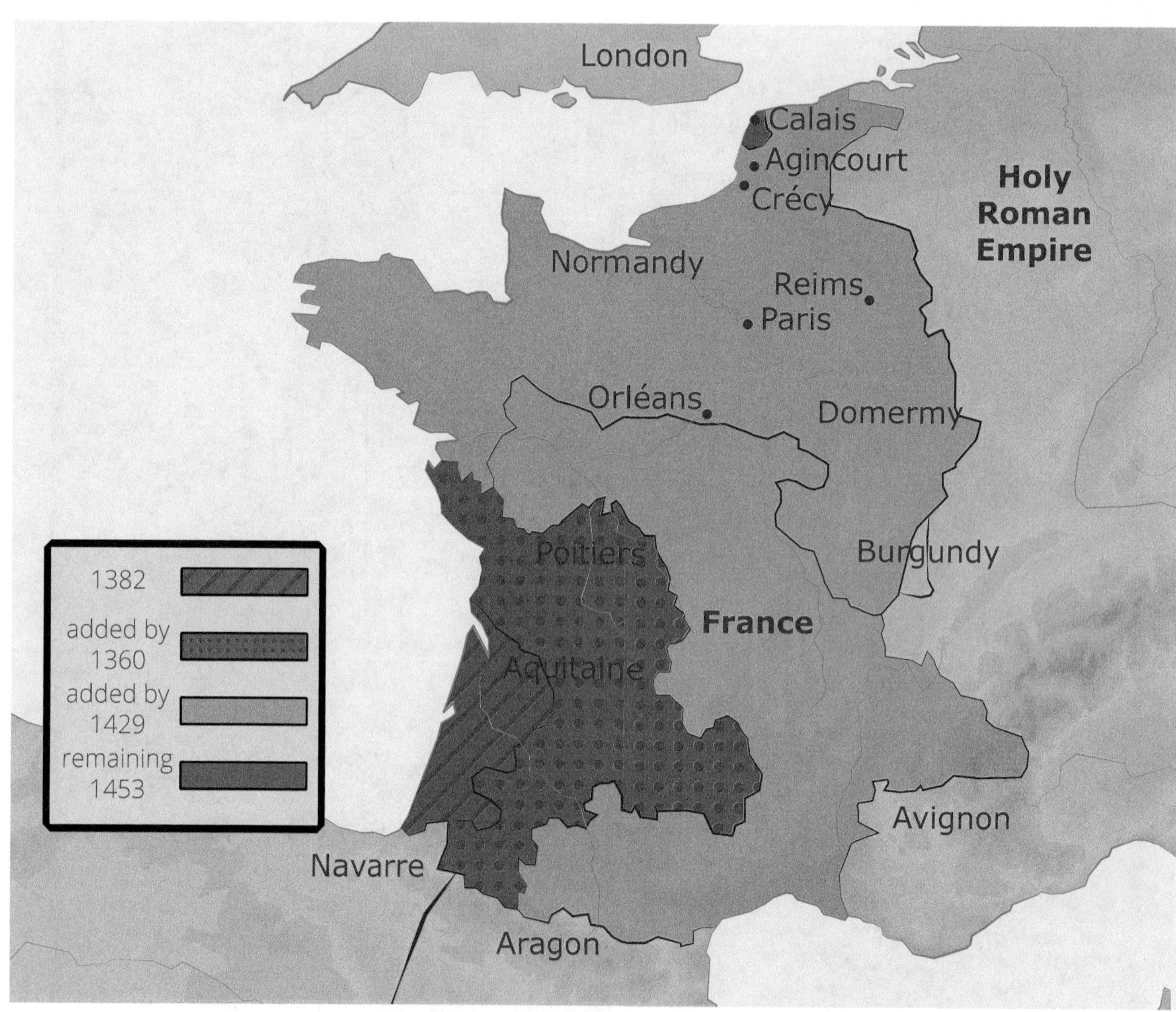

| English Possession in France during the Hundred Years' War 1337-1453

The war effort, which in fact had not stopped, was renewed by Charles V in 1369. The French, led by Bertrand du Guesclin, were at a definite advantage. France was aided by the Spanish fleet. As a result, the English agreed to another truce, which lasted until the death of Edward III in 1377.

Richard II of England inherited the crown as a child. His incompetent counselors were unable to pull the country together to resist renewed coastal attacks by the French.

During Charles' reign, the tax system became more efficient. The French monarchy was supported by a tax structure that brought in more money than that of any other European power.

In 1380 both General du Guesclin and Charles V died. Charles VI, called Charles the Mad, was not old enough to rule. His uncles, who were selfishly acting in their behalf, were unable to unite the factions in France. By 1394, a truce was signed with England, and in 1396, Richard II married the daughter of Charles VI. The result of this alliance was peace with England for about thirty years.

France, however, was plunged into a period of civil strife because illness had left Charles VI insane. France had no strong central government such as England had in Parliament. The *Parlement* of Paris was a law court and the *Estates General* was almost nonexistent. Two contenders for power were Philip the Bold, the Duke of Burgundy and the uncle of Charles VI, and Louis, the Duke of Orléans and the brother of Charles VI. After Philip's death in 1404, his son, John the Fearless, had Louis murdered. A few years later, Duke John was himself assassinated.

By 1415, Henry V had invaded France and gained a victory. The Treaty of Troyes was signed in 1420. France was still a divided country.

Joan of Arc, a young girl from Domremy, furthered the cause of French nationalism. Joan had absorbed the people's feelings of resentment against the English occupation and civil disorder. The legendary and historical aspects of the story of Joan of Arc are intertwined. Both affected a twenty-year period of history.

Joan had heard voices and had seen visions as an adolescent. She believed she had been visited by the archangel Michael, who instructed her to become "an instrument of divine will." Whatever her motivation, she set out to help the king receive his rightful crown and kingdom by driving out the English and subduing the opposition. Joan convinced Charles VII of her divine mission, and she was allowed to accompany troops to relieve the troops of the besieged Orléans. With her help, the French troops promptly defeated the English along the Loire.

Joan decided that Charles should be crowned at Rheims, which was held by the English. Therefore, French troops stormed through the English-held territory. In 1429 Charles was crowned in an extremely simple ceremony. With the crowning of a king, the national spirit of the people arose.

Feeling that her goal had been accomplished, Joan wished to return home. Charles, however, refused to let her go. After a military setback, Joan of Arc was captured in 1430 by the English, who sent her to the Inquisition. She was tried as a witch and a heretic and was burned at the stake in 1431.

The French forces rallied and a period of negotiation followed. By 1436, the capital and most of France had been restored to Charles VII, known as the Well Served. France emerged from the Hundred Years' War a national power, supported by people desiring protection from war and lawlessness.

Louis XI became king of France in 1461, succeeding Charles VII. He was a monarch used to getting his own way by whatever means it might take. He would use diplomacy, bribery, and even poison. One stumbling block for Louis XI was Charles the Bold of Burgundy. In an effort to increase his own power, Charles was killed. Louis then seized Burgundy. France also captured Provence and Brittany. By the end of the fifteenth century, France had become a strong monarchy. It had a strongly centralized administration and a royally controlled judicial system. Under France's system, the nobility played a secondary role to the king, but the **bourgeoisie** had risen in importance.

KINGS OF FRANCE

ROYAL HOUSE	REIGNING NAME	EPITHET OR NOTABLE ACT	REIGN AS KING
House of Capet	Louis IX	*"Saint Louis"*	(1226-1270)
	Philip III	*The "Bold"*	(1270-1285)
	Philip IV	*The "Fair"*	(1285-1314)
	Louis X	*The "Stubborn"*	(1314-1316)
	John I	Died in Infancy	(1316)
	Philip V	*The "Tall"*	(1316-1322)
	Charles IV	*The "Fair"*	(1322-1328)
House of Valois	Philip VI	*The "Fortunate"*	(1328-1350)
	John II	*The "Good"*	(1350-1364)
	Charles V	*The "Wise"*	(1364-1380)
	Charles VI	*The "Mad"*	(1380-1422)
	Charles VII	*The "Victorious"*	(1422-1461)
	Louis XI	*The "Spider"*	(1461-1483)
	Charles VIII	*The "Affable"*	(1483-1498)
	Louis XII	*"The Father of the People"*	(1498-1515)
	Francis I	Standardized the French Language	(1515-1547)
	Henry II		(1547-1559)
	Francis II		(1559-1560)
	Charles IX		(1560-1574)
	Henry III	King of Poland-Lithuania before France	(1574-1589)
House of Burbon	Henry IV	*"Good King Henry"*	(1589-1610)
	Louis XIII	*The "Just"*	(1610-1643)
	Louis XIV	*The "Great" or "The Sun King"*	(1643-1715)

Complete the following activities.

1.1 What was the Renaissance?

____

____

____

1.2 List four reasons for the Renaissance.

a. ____

b. ____

c. ____

d. ____

1.3 List four major areas of change.

a. ____

b. ____

c. ____

d. ____

Write the letter for the correct answer on each blank.

1.4 One factor *not* leading to the Hundred Years' War was ______ .

a. England's trade with Flanders
b. English possession of French territory
c. The marriage between Richard II and the daughter of Charles VI
d. French alliance with Scotland against England

1.5 Bertrand Du Guesclin was the ______ .

a. French advisor to Scotland
b. French general under Charles V
c. Count of Flanders, a French fief
d. leader of the French sailors

1.6 Flanders was important as ______ .

a. a French fief
b. a strategically located town on the English Channel
c. Du Guesclin's duchy
d. a center for weaving woolen cloth

1.7 The fact that was *not* true of France during the period before 1364 is that ______ .
a. France was a strong national power
b. France had a weak government
c. France suffered military devastation
d. the war ended temporarily with the Treaty of Calais

1.8 The reign of Charles V did *not* bring about ______ .
a. a lasting peace
b. the elimination of governmental corruption
c. the establishment of France as a strong nation
d. an efficient tax structure bringing in more money than that of any alien European power

Complete the following statements.

1.9 Joan of Arc believed in a strong ______________________________ .

1.10 In a simple ceremony, ______________________________ was crowned king of France.

1.11 Joan was captured, sent to the Inquisition, and ______________________________ .

1.12 France emerged from the Hundred Years' War as a ______________________________ .

1.13 Charles VII was succeeded by ______________________________ .

England. Before the reign of Edward III, England was weakened by the differing factions. Edward II was opposed by barons who were afraid of a powerful monarchy. They forced the king to grant them powers of reform in 1311. The ordinances they made reorganized the government, giving it greater power. They removed all opponents from power and forbade the king to act without their approval. The king, accused of neglect and incompetence, was deposed from the throne and subsequently was murdered. Although the actions of the barons were selfish in motive, the result of these actions were forerunners of a representative system of parliamentary government.

Edward III brought unity to England. The barons caused him to restore Archbishop Stratford, who had been removed from office, to his position as chancellor. The conflict between the barons and the royalty almost disappeared during his reign. Edward was a popular monarch. He was energetic, ambitious, gracious, and responsive to the people. The middle class began to become more influential during Edward's reign. His major contribution to the unity of England was to prevent domestic strife by becoming involved in foreign affairs. The Hundred Years' War, which began during Edward's reign in 1337 and continued until 1453, was dominated by English victories until the 1420s when France began to win significant battles and finally won the war.

Edward III was a popular king and the war was welcomed by the English people. The English had utilized the longbow and the pike successfully in many battles. The Black Death, or plague, of 1348 and 1349, delayed the war for a time. Economic problems were magnified by unemployed, unskilled veterans. During this period of domestic unrest, Parliament became more important, especially as a source of levying revenue.

By the mid-fourteenth century, groups of knights and burgesses had begun meeting to discuss common problems or to write petitions to submit to the king's council. From this consultation grew the House of Commons, which gained control over taxation and other matters, limiting the king's powers. As a result of the growth of power, the House of Commons gained the right to impeach certain royal ministers on charges of misconduct. The House of Lords, in turn, decided the innocence or guilt of the accused.

Richard II, young successor of Edward III, was surrounded by plots. Domestic struggles ensued and, as an outgrowth of this discontent, the Peasants' Revolt occurred in 1381. Both the Archbishop of Canterbury and the treasurer were assassinated, but the rebels finally were subdued.

Richard II set out to provide a strong monarchy, but lost the support of both the nobles and the middle class. As a result of Richard's unlawful confiscation of Lancaster, Henry of Lancaster, with his men, captured the king and claimed the crown. Parliament met to affirm Henry IV as king. Parliament's very usefulness preserved its existence during the fourteenth and fifteenth centuries.

Henry IV suppressed several rebellions, but his son Henry V, beset by domestic strife, diverted the rebellious forces to France. The English, under Henry's rule, won several important victories. In 1420, Henry V married Catherine, daughter of Charles VI, uniting France and England. Henry V died in 1422.

Henry VI was a baby when he succeeded his father. His representatives quarreled among themselves, resulting in a weakening of England's position in France. By 1453, the English had lost all French positions except Calais.

The Wars of the Roses, a domestic conflict between the Yorkists and the Lancastrians, broke out in 1455. The term *Wars of the Roses* grew out of the emblems of the opposing forces. The emblem of the Yorkists was a white rose, and the emblem of the Lancastrians was a red rose. The two houses were struggling over the claim to the throne. King Henry VI claimed the throne through the male descendants of Edward III; the Yorkist dukes claimed the throne through the female line.

In 1483 Edward of York defeated Henry VI. Edward, who reigned as Edward IV from 1461 until 1483, brought a strong rule to England. He had to squelch uprisings, one of which resulted in the temporary crowning of Henry VI. Henry was subsequently murdered and Edward reigned until his death, when his son became King Edward V.

Almost immediately, Edward IV's brother, Richard, the duke of Gloucester, claimed the throne after condemning his nephews, Edward V and his younger brother, Richard, as being illegitimate. He had the brothers arrested and imprisoned in the Tower of London. No one knows exactly what happened to them after that, but they were probably murdered, possibly by their uncle. Parliament was required to legalize Richard III's claim to the throne.

In 1485 Richard III fell to the sword of Henry Tudor. Through his mother, Henry claimed right to the throne. He united Yorkist and Lancastrian claims by marrying one of Edward IV's daughters. Henry VII used subtle means to rid himself of his enemies. Henry allowed them to plot against him, then exposed them. The Star Chamber, which he created, held secret trials to convict enemies of the government. Through Martin, one of Henry's ministers, Henry VII collected a vast amount of money. Since its aid in obtaining money was not needed, Parliament seldom met; therefore a more powerful monarchy developed.

The Tudor dynasty eventually brought about a period of peace and prosperity, lasting over one hundred years. Growing out of the apparent chaos of the fifteenth century, strong elements of a centralized government and a sound economy evolved.

ENGLISH MONARCHS			
ROYAL HOUSE	**REIGNING NAME**	**EPITHET OR NOTABLE ACT**	**REIGN AS MONARCH**
House of Plantaget	**Edward I**	*"Longshanks"*	(1272-1307)
	Edward II		(1307-1327)
	Edward III	Revolutionized the English Military and Government	(1327-1377)
	Richard II	Overthrown then Imprisoned	(1377-1399)
House of Lancaster	**Henry IV**	Dealt with many rebellions	(1399-1413)
	Henry V	*"The Star of England"*	(1413-1422)
	Henry VI	Deposed then Restored	(1422-1461) and (1470-1471)
House of York	**Edward IV**	Deposed then Restored	(1461-1470) and (1471-1483)
	Edward V		(1483)
	Richard III	Last English King to Die in battle	(1483-1485)
House of Tudor	**Henry VII**	Last English king to win the crown through battle	(1485-1509)
	Henry VIII	Founded Anglican Church	(1509-1547)
	Edward VI	Died at age 15	(1547-1553)
	Mary I	*"Bloody Mary"*	(1553-1558)
	Elizabeth I	Patron of the Arts	(1558-1603)

Answer true or false.

1.14 ____________ The barons who deposed Edward II because they feared a strong monarchy paved the way for a parliamentary government.

1.15 ____________ The middle class became more important during the rule of Edward III.

1.16 ____________ Edward III's major contribution was to restore Archbishop Stratford as chancellor.

1.17 ____________ The Hundred Years' War lasted over a century.

1.18 ____________ Although the French won most of the battles after 1350, the English won the war.

1.19 ____________ Henry VI was the young successor of Edward III.

1.20 ____________ Edward V escaped from the tower and claimed the throne from the duke of Gloucester.

1.21 ____________ The Tudor dynasty brought over one hundred years of peace and prosperity.

Italy. During the fourteenth century, the Renaissance began in the strife-torn country of Italy. As a result of political and religious struggles between the Holy Roman emperors, the papacy, and other factions, regionalism, rather than nationalism, prevailed during the fourteenth and fifteenth centuries. This regionalistic tendency led to the development of the city-states into five major states: the Republic of Venice, the Duchy of Milan, the Republic of Florence, the Papal States, and the Kingdom of Naples.

The Republic of Venice, the most politically stable of the five states, was the wealthiest Italian state, because it controlled Mediterranean commerce. Venice had a state fleet of more than three thousand ships and a huge arsenal that produced ship parts, cannons, and other related products.

Venice was controlled by a *doge*, or duke who was a figure elected by the Great Council which consisted of about two hundred wealthy merchants. The Council of Ten wielded the actual powers of the state. Venice had the most efficient government in Italy, with its diplomatic service and official poisoner, who was used to rid the state of enemies. The church was also dominated by the governor.

The Duchy of Milan, also a wealthy state, manufactured silks, woolens, and armor. Because of its location, the Duchy of Milan was both a commercially important trade center and an agriculturally self-sufficient producer of food. Tyrants of the aristocracy dominated it politically. The duchy included a large portion of northern Italy. At the death of the last VisConti ruler, Milan was proclaimed a republic.

Almost immediately, Francisco Sforza took over the duchy, bringing progress to Milan. He achieved independence and peace through diplomacy. After the turn of the sixteenth century, Milan fell under Spanish rule.

The Republic of Florence, the second wealthiest Italian state, based its economy on textile factories, flourishing trade, and outstanding banking houses. Florence controlled Pisa, providing access to the Mediterranean. Florence provided the standard gold coin of Europe—the *florin*. Florence was actually an oligarchy, a government ruled by only a privileged few. Florence's government was controlled by seven major guilds representing bankers, merchants, and manufacturers. Only members of these seven major guilds and fourteen minor ones had the right to vote.

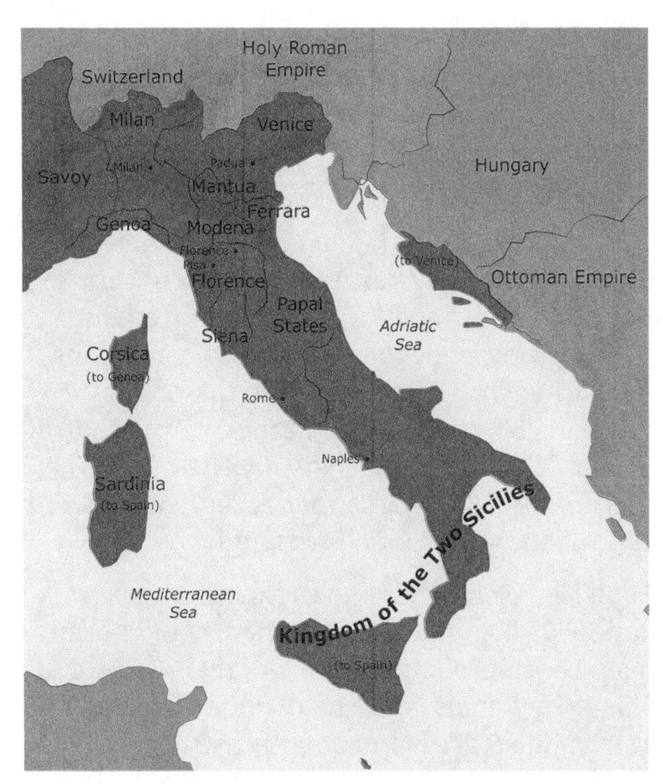

| Italian City-States in 1494

Several wealthy families struggled over power, but the Medici family actually ruled without holding office. For a period of over three hundred years, they were the most powerful political force in Florence. Cosimo de' Medici, the first Medici ruler, was the richest banker in Florence. Lorenzo, the Magnificent, was the most famous Medici. By 1530 the Medici family officially became hereditary rulers, combining Florence and the surrounding area into the Duchy of Tuscany.

The Renaissance, which began in Florence, was financially encouraged and supported by the Medicis and its chief patrons. Such Renaissance artists as Giotto, Botticelli, Leonardo da Vinci, and Michelangelo were products of Florence.

With the coming of the Renaissance, some of the popes virtually became worldly princes. They sponsored the Renaissance movement, granting privileges to relatives and conducting wars. The Papal States, given to the popes by Pepin in 751, consisted of Rome and the central portion of the Italian peninsula. The papacy had lost control over secular affairs, which were controlled by individual lords and tyrants.

Pope Nicholas V founded the Vatican library. Pope Pius II, a multitalented man, could have been considered an example of the *universal man*—the Renaissance ideal. Pope Sixtus IV, patron of Botticelli and other artists, encouraged Rome's architectural improvement. He sponsored the building of the Sistine Chapel.

Other popes increased papal authority by subjugating local rulers through such violent methods as murder and treachery. Cesare Borgia, Pope Alexander VI's ruthless son, was the model for Machiavelli's *The Prince*. Pope Julius II ended Cesare Borgia's career and militarily restored papal authority. Sponsoring Michelangelo and Raphael brought a golden age to Rome.

A Florentine Dominican friar named Savonarola denounced the elements of paganism and worldliness exhibited in Florence. A forerunner of the Reformation, Savonarola established himself as dictator. Pope Alexander VI excommunicated him for attacking the church. Savonarola attacked the pope verbally, was tried for heresy, and was hanged in 1498.

The Kingdom of Naples was ruled by the French until 1435 when the Spanish seized control. Ferdinand I allied with Florence and Milan. After his reign, the French invaded Italy in 1495. Nine years later the Spanish seized control.

Identify or define the following terms.

1.22 doge ____

1.23 oligarchy ____

1.24 Savonarola ____

____

1.25 Great Council ____

____

1.26 Francisco Sforza ____

1.27 De' Medici ____

____

1.28 florin ____

Match the correct term on the left with characteristics on the right.

1.29 _______ The Republic of Venice

1.30 _______ The Duchy of Milan

1.31 _______ The Republic of Florence

1.32 _______ The Papal States

1.33 _______ The Kingdom of Naples

a. consisted of Rome and the central portion of the Italian peninsula

b. was the wealthiest and most politically stable of the Italian states

c. was under French rule until Spain took over

d. was the scene of the Wars of the Roses

e. was an important banking center, governed by seven major guilds

f. manufactured silks, woolens, and armor

KINGS OF SPAIN			
ROYAL HOUSE	**REIGNING NAME**	**EPITHET OR NOTABLE ACT**	**REIGNED AS KING**
House of Trastámara	**Ferdinand of Aragon and Isabella of Castile**	United the crowns of the Iberian Peninsula	1479-1504
	Ferdinand of Aragon	Acting regent for his daughter then grandson	1504-1516
House of Hapsburg	**Charles I**	Also reigned as Holy Roman Emperor	1516-1556
	Philip II	*"The Prudent"*	1556-1598
	Philip III	*"The Pious"*	1598-1621
	Philip IV	*"The Great"*	1621-1665
	Charles II	*"The Bewitched"*	1665-1700
House of Bourbon	**Philip V**	*"The Spirited"*	1700-1746

Spain. The Muslim Caliphate had declined and the Christian states of the Iberian peninsula had emerged by the end of the tenth century. During the eleventh century and part of the twelfth, these states grew in importance. The Christians drove out many of the **Moors** who had occupied the southern areas of Spain. This movement was called the *Reconquista*, or reconquest. By 1140 Christian Spain consisted of three parts: Castile and Leon, Portugal, and Aragon.

In 1146 the Almohads, a new Muslim power originating in Africa, renewed the fighting. Enemies tended to be poorly defined, resulting in the fighting of Christian against Christian and Moor against Moor. By the thirteenth century the Almohads seemed to be winning. A special crusade was sent out by Innocent III, resulting in the defeat of the Almohads in 1212 at *Las Navas de Tolosa*.

Ferdinand III from Castile joined James I, the conqueror of Aragon, in another reconquest effort. Because of the military efforts of these two armies combined with the internal quarrels of the Almohads, only Granada remained a Moorish possession by 1270. Things remained relatively static until the reign of Ferdinand and Isabella, despite internal struggles.

The powers of the monarchy were intensified by national unity against the Moors. When Ferdinand of Aragon married Isabella of Castile, a greater national unity was achieved. During their reign a royal police force, known as a "holy brotherhood," restored civil peace. The Spanish treasuries were filled by payments for privileges that some of the nobles had taken from the crown.

Under Ferdinand and Isabella, the Spanish Inquisition—a form of church court—was established, Granada was recaptured, and

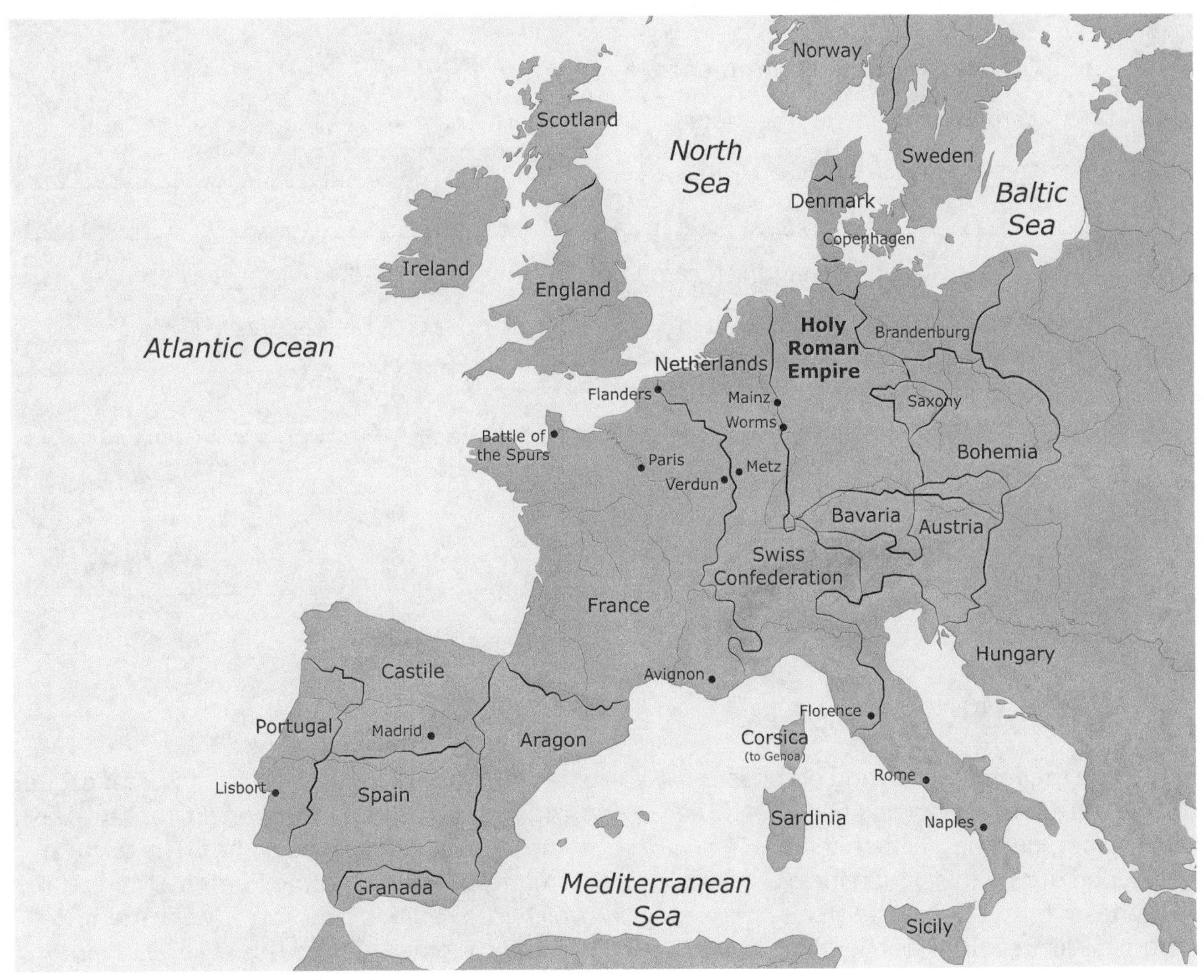

| European Nations of the Sixteenth Century

the Moors and Jews were either converted or expelled. For the first time, a unity existed among the people of Spain. A political Spanish unity similar to that of England was impossible. Spain, however, did achieve a unity of faith and of territory. During Ferdinand and Isabella's reign the beginnings of a world power were established. Spanish influence through trade and expansion began with the discovery of America by Christopher Columbus, whose expedition was financed by Spain.

Complete the following statements.

1.34 The movement to drive out the Moors from southern Spain was called ____________________.

1.35 The three parts which made up Christian Spain in 1140 were a. ____________________, b. ____________________, and c. ____________________.

1.36 In 1146 a new Muslim power which came out of Africa was called ____________________.

1.37 A great national unity was achieved in Spain with the marriage between a. ____________________ of Aragon and b. ____________________ of Castile.

1.38 Four accomplishments Ferdinand and Isabella achieved were a. ____________________, b. ____________________, c. ____________________, and d. ____________________.

1.39 The Spanish achieved a unity of a. ____________________ and of b. ____________________.

DEVELOPMENTS IN ART

Art during the medieval period emphasized architecture rather than painting. The three major types, or styles, of architecture that developed during this period included Gothic, Romanesque, and Byzantine architecture. Moorish architecture was a less important type used primarily in southern Spain. The Alhambra is probably the best known example of Moorish architecture.

Architecture. *Gothic* architecture, characterized by its vaulted arches, horizontal lines, elaborate carvings, and stained glass windows, is seen in many of the famous European cathedrals. Built in the shape of a cross, the medieval cathedrals have beautiful stained glass windows—sometimes round rose windows—pointed arches, towers, steeples, or spires, and slender external beams called flying buttresses that give external support to the cathedral. One of the most famous Gothic cathedrals is Notre Dame in Paris.

Romanesque architecture, used in the eleventh, twelfth, and thirteenth centuries, emphasized strength in its massiveness. Most Romanesque buildings were heavily supported, thick-walled structures with low, wide arches. The term Romanesque refers to the Roman architecture which inspired this later form. Many monasteries and churches utilized this style. Dark and gloomy, these buildings varied somewhat from country to country. Some of the more famous examples of Romanesque architecture include the Cathedral at Worms, Germany; the Leaning Tower of Pisa, Italy; and the Angouleme Cathedral in France.

Byzantine architecture, an outgrowth of the Roman basilica, flourished from the fifth century A.D. to the mid-fifteenth-century. Byzantine churches were characterized by complex domes and vaults atop square or rectangular structures. Ornate mosaics and colorful paintings covered the church interiors. The exteriors were also usually ornate and colorful. Saint Basil's Church in Moscow and the Hagia Sophia's Church in Constantinople are uniquely beautiful examples of this exotic architectural style.

The Renaissance, which began in Italy and spread throughout the countries of Europe during the fifteenth and sixteenth centuries, brought about architectural changes. Many of the earlier medieval styles were modified or combined into new forms. Saint Peter's church in Rome was worked on by several outstanding Renaissance artists and architects including Michelangelo, who designed the dome. Renaissance architects designed houses, public buildings, and palaces, as well as churches. Inigo Jones (1573-1652) designed such English buildings as the Queen's House at Greenwich, London. These Renaissance styles developed into a baroque, or exaggerated elaborate style, by the seventeenth century.

Painting. Painting during the medieval period had been very simple and, at times, stiff and artificial. In thirteenth-century Italy, Giotto's paintings provided the transition between the Middle Ages and the Renaissance. He utilized an illusion of depth to produce a sense of real people and real space. His frescoes showed a naturalism which served as a model for other Renaissance painters and sculptors. Masaccio, another Florentine painter, contributed the use of perspective, the realistic painting of the human figure, and the experimentation with *chiaroscuro*—a technique of painting shadow.

Botticelli developed an almost ethereal style of painting idealized subjects usually from classical mythology. He later concentrated on religious subjects as a result of Savonarola's influences.

Leonardo da Vinci epitomized the *universal man* of the Renaissance. Although best-known as a painter, he was also skilled in anatomy, architecture, botany, engineering, mathematics, physiology, and sculpture. Da Vinci's "The Last Supper" eloquently portrays the faces of the Apostles at the moment of Christ's announcement of his impending betrayal. The "Mona Lisa" and "The Virgin, St. Anne, and the Infant Jesus" are other outstanding paintings by da Vinci. Da Vinci's sketches of early airplanes, tanks, and parachutes indicate a mind far ahead of its time.

Michelangelo, often considered the greatest artist of all times, was not only a painter and sculptor. He was also an architect, engineer, and poet. Michelangelo completed the momentous task of painting almost three hundred fifty fresco figures on the ceiling of the Sistine Chapel. This masterpiece of over one hundred panels, depicts such scenes from Genesis as the "Creation of Adam." The painting "The Last Judgment" appears on the altar wall of the Sistine Chapel. As a sculptor, Michelangelo produced the "Pietá," "David," and "Moses. "

Raphael blended classical culture and Christianity. Raphael, with da Vinci and Michelangelo, was one of the three greatest Renaissance painters. Raphael's most famous painting is the "Sistine Madonna." Another painting, "The School of Athens," portrays the great philosophers. Raphael caused portrait painting to achieve new heights of popularity.

Other Italian painters included Bellini and his pupils Giorgione and Titian. This group, known as the *Venetian school of paintings*, used oil colors, rather than water tempera colors.

In other areas of Europe, painting flourished as well. The Flemish school of painting included Jan and Hubert van Eyck. Pieter Brueghel, the Elder, was also a Flemish painter. Unlike the Van Eycks who painted three-dimensional figures and religious themes, Brueghel concentrated on landscapes and scenes of common life. "The Harvesters" is one of his realistic peasant scenes.

Two German painters include Albrecht Dürer, who led the German Renaissance school of painting, and Hans Holbein, the Younger, who was court painter to Henry VII in England. Dürer was most famous for his engravings, and Holbein was famous for portraits and wood cuts. Holbein painted the famous portraits of *Henry VIII* and *Sir Thomas More*.

Two Renaissance artists in Spain include Murillo and Velazquez. Murillo is known for his *St. Anthony of Padua*. Velazquez studied in Rome, then returned to Madrid to the court of Philip IV. His portraits of the royal family depict the lifestyle and personalities of the Spanish. Some of his famous paintings include *Las Meninas*, a scene of the Court Studio; *The Water-Seller of Seville*; and *Prince Philip Prosper of Spain*, a charming portrait of the two-year-old prince and his dog.

Complete the following activities.

1.40 List three major styles of medieval architecture: a. ______________________,
b. ______________________, and c. ______________________.

1.41 Notre Dame in Paris is a famous cathedral built in the ______________________ style.

1.42 The dark, rather gloomy style of architecture utilizing low, wide arches is called ______________________.

1.43 One example of brightly colored churches with complex domes and vaults is ______________________.

1.44 Two Renaissance architects who designed churches and other structures were
a. ______________________ and b. ______________________.

Match the artist with his technique or to his work. Some artists may be used more than once.

1.45 ________ the illusion of depth

1.46 ________ perspective and *chiaroscuro*

1.47 ________ "The Last Supper"

1.48 ________ "Sistine Madonna"

1.49 ________ "David"

1.50 ________ "Mona Lisa"

1.51 ________ early airplanes

1.52 ________ portrait of Henry VIII

1.53 ________ Flemish painter

1.54 ________ Spanish painter

1.55 ________ frescoes on the ceiling of the Sistine Chapel

a. Masaccio
b. Raphael
c. Michelangelo
d. Holbein
e. Giotto
f. da Vinci
g. van Eyck
h. Velazquez

Complete the following statements.

1.56 Art during the Renaissance became more ____ .

1.57 Most Renaissance painters chose ____ subjects.

1.58 The man who most closely approached the ideal of a universal man was ________________ .

1.59 The Venetian school of painting used ___________________________ rather than tempera.

1.60 An artist famous for his engravings was ____ .

CHANGES IN LITERATURE AND THOUGHT

Beginning in Italy and spreading through Spain, France, northern Europe, and England, many changes occurred in literature and thought. The changes were aided by new inventions, especially the printing press.

Italian writers. A new learning developed in Italy in the fourteenth century through the works of Petrarch. Often called the "Father of Humanism," Petrarch tried to spread an interest in the study of the classics. He has been called the first "modern man" because of his interest in the **humanities** and because of his methods, which differed greatly from those of medieval scholars. Petrarch encouraged Boccaccio to translate Homer's *Iliad* into Latin. Petrarch wrote over three hundred love sonnets, which were imitated by European poets. Petrarch was the first modern **poet laureate**.

Boccaccio was the Renaissance storyteller, writing what may be called Europe's first psychological novel. Some of his writings, although somewhat pagan and romantic in spirit, provided models for some of Chaucer's tales. *The Decameron* was his masterpiece.

Marsilio Ficino, during the fifteenth century, first used the term *platonic* love, a pure idealized love leading to God. He synthesized the doctrines of Christian theology and the concepts of Plato. This blending of **Christian humanism** with these doctrines resulted in **Neoplatonism**.

Niccolo Machiavelli was a diplomat, dramatist, historian, and poet who dreamed of unifying Italy. He wrote a manual for rulers called *The Prince*, which encouraged unethical tactics. The idea expressed was that "the end justifies the means." Because of his realistic look at politics, Machiavelli might be considered the father of modern political science.

Other Italian Renaissance works include *The Autobiography of Benvenuto Cellini*. Cellini was burned at the stake for expressing his agreement with Copernicus and Galileo that the sun was the center of our solar system.

Northern European writers. In northern Europe the humanists utilized the teachings of early Christianity. This movement, known as Christian humanism, attempted to restore a purity to Christianity. Reforms within the church were their aim. Erasmus was known as the greatest scholar of Europe. Born in Rotterdam in the Netherlands, he studied in Italy and Paris. A former Augustinian monk, he taught in England and finally spent the rest of his life studying in Switzerland. Erasmus' writings exemplified exactness and thoroughness. *The Praise of Folly*, written to portray man's nature and the problems in the church, is a satire. In *The Praise of Folly*, Erasmus ridiculed man's interest in war and the church's sale of indulgences.

French writers. French writers of the Renaissance include Francois Villon, who was actually a transitional part of the fifteenth century; Pierre de Ronsard, the chief poet of the French Renaissance; Joacin de Bellay; and Francois Rabelais. Rabelais was both a Franciscan and a Benedictine monk. He was also a Christian humanist, a physician, and a scholar. He wrote satires on medieval institutions and beliefs. Rabelais believed in the benefits of education. Montaigne, another French scholar, developed the personal essay as a new type of literary form. His *Essays* influenced later writers.

English writers. England produced many Renaissance writers. Sir Thomas More, an outstanding Christian humanist, wrote *Utopia*. More also attacked money, the new capitalism in England, and the landlord class. Another writer, Francis Bacon, wrote *The New Atlantis*, which also described an idealized world. Bacon was an essayist and a scientist. Although the Renaissance was late coming to England, it flourished during the Elizabethan Age. Sir Philip Sidney, Edmund Spenser, and Michael Drayton were outstanding Elizabethan poets.

English drama achieved prominence with the works of Christopher Marlowe and William Shakespeare, who is considered the greatest literary figure in the English language. Among Shakespeare's thirty-eight known plays are the tragedies of *Hamlet, Macbeth, Othello*, and *Romeo and Juliet*; the comedies include *As You Like It, A Midsummer Night's Dream, The Taming of the Shrew*, and *The Merchant of Venice*; and such histories as *The Tragedy of King Richard II* and *The Life of King Henry* V. Shakespeare also wrote lyric poetry.

Ben Jonson was a neoclassicist. Resisting romantic style, Jonson wrote satiric comedies. He was both a dramatist and a poet. "Song to Celia" is his most famous *lyric* poem.

Spanish writers. Spanish writers of the Renaissance include poets, dramatists, and novelists. The most outstanding dramatist of the period was Lope de Vega, who had served in the Spanish Armada, had been a priest, and had been a member of the government. His plays were usually about historical or religious subjects. He also wrote a type of adventure drama, known as *cape y espada*, or cloak and sword (dagger). These plays had imaginative plots with realistic treatment of Spanish customs and traditions.

Miguel de Cervantes was the most outstanding contributor to Spanish literature. His *Don Quixote de la Mancha* (Don Quixote) was a satire about chivalry.

Inventions. One major invention of this period made literature more readily available to poets and to the people. This invention was the printing press. The earliest printing press used in Europe before the fifteenth century used carved wooden blocks. Since this method of printing was so time consuming, relatively little material was printed until the invention of movable type. Johann Gutenberg is generally credited with its invention. He used movable type to publish a Bible in 1456. This invention was quickly adopted by European printers. By the turn of the sixteenth century, over two hundred printers were using movable type.

Paper, which had been devised in China, was manufactured and exported by the Muslims in the Middle Ages. Since it was an inexpensive substitute for parchment, printers began to use a great quantity of paper. Soon Europeans began to manufacture paper, causing the cost of printing books to be relatively low.

Various styles of type were developed by European printers. Books at last were available to the public. Previously hand-printed copies had been too expensive for the average person to buy, since an average book took around six months to copy by hand. The development of movable type encouraged the spread of learning during the Renaissance.

Write the letter for the correct answer on each blank.

1.61 The man who tried to spread an interest in the classics was ______ .
a. Machiavelli b. Chaucer c. Petrarch d. Montaigne

1.62 The author of what might be called Europe's first psychological novel was ______ .
a. Homer b. Boccaccio c. Petrarch d. Plato

1.63 The man who first used the term *platonic* love was ______ .
a. Ficino b. Cellini c. Petrarch d. Bruno

1.64 The author of *The Prince* which justifies many unethical practices in politics was ______ .
a. Machiavelli b. Cellini c. Ficino d. Benvenuto

1.65 Erasmus' *The Praise of Folly* is ______ .
a. *lyric* poetry b. a satire c. an autobiography d. a political manual

Complete the following statements.

1.66 Two Englishmen who wrote about an idealized world were a. ______________________________ and b. ______________________________ .

1.67 Three outstanding Elizabethan poets were a. ______________________________ , b. ______________________________ , and c. ______________________________ .

1.68 The greatest literary figure in the English language was a. ______________________________ who wrote three types of plays: b. ____________________ , c. ____________________ , and d. ____________________ .

1.69 A neoclassicist who wrote satiric comedies was ______________________________ .

1.70 Lope de Vega wrote *cape y espada* or ______________________________ plays.

1.71 Miguel de Cervantes is best known for his ______________________________ .

ADVANCES IN SCIENCE

The Middle Ages marks the beginning of modern science. Various elements of investigation, study, and thought, coupled with new inventions and discoveries brought about advances in science. The alchemists of this period were attempting to derive gold from other elements.

Mathematical ideas were adopted from Arabian concepts. Astronomy was actually astrology during the Renaissance. Superstition and fortune telling dominated this area of investigations. The theory of Ptolemy, set forth in the second century, was still accepted by scientists of the Middle Ages. They believed that the earth was the center of the universe and that all the heavens revolved around it. Science made great advances with the discoveries and inventions of such men as Bacon, da Vinci, Copernicus, Galileo, Kepler, and Newton.

Roger Bacon. Roger Bacon, a thirteenth-century scholar, believed in experimentation, rather than in a simple reasoning process. In his book, *Opus Majus*, Bacon described spectacles, or eyeglasses, which became popular toward the end of the Middle Ages.

Leonardo da Vinci. Although many people classify the contributions of Leonardo da Vinci among the arts, some of his most interesting ideas occurred in the fields of science. These fields included anatomy, botany, engineering, geology, and astronomy. His works reveal intricately detailed studies of bone and muscle. Other sketches show men "flying" with man-made "wings." Da Vinci's designs involve primitive prototypes for the helicopter, the parachute, the machine gun, armored tanks, and other machines. Da Vinci also made geological studies of rock formations and water movement. He developed canal systems complete with locks, as a part of his job to divert rivers. Because of his versatility and genius, da Vinci is considered today to be the standing representative of the ideal Renaissance man.

| Nicolaus Copernicus

Copernicus. By the mid-sixteenth century, a Polish priest named Nicolaus Copernicus had published *On the Revolution of Heavenly Bodies*, an assertion that the sun was the center of the universe, or that the universe was **heliocentric**. A scholarly man with a doctor's degree, Copernicus believed that the earth moved through the universe and was just one of the several planets.

Although most of the Renaissance people refused to accept this new theory, his heliocentric theory influenced the other scientific developments by Galileo, Johannes Kepler, and later by Sir Isaac Newton.

Galileo. Galileo was an Italian scientist who at the turn of the seventeenth century made several important scientific discoveries. Galileo developed a way for determining the specific gravity of objects and discovered the laws of the pendulum. He also invented a type of compass that is still used by draftsmen.

Galileo is known primarily for his discoveries in the field of astronomy. His development of bigger and better telescopes enabled him to observe the heavens more closely. Galileo discovered that the moon did not generate its own light, but that light was reflected by a rough, mountainous surface. He also discovered four of Jupiter's satellites, naming them for members of the famous Medici family. Other astronomical discoveries, including sunspots and observations of phases of Venus, brought him fame as well as opposition from the church. After the publication of his *A Dialogue on the Two Principle Systems of the World*, Galileo was called before the Inquisition and publicly forced to deny the Copernican theory.

Johannes Kepler. Johannes Kepler, who lived at the same time as Galileo, publicly supported the Copernican theory. A German scientist and mathematician, Kepler made valuable contributions to the field of astronomy. He worked with Tycho Brahe, an earlier astronomer who had made many observations of the planet Mars unaided by telescope. While investigating Brahe's theories, Kepler discovered that the orbit of Mars was oval, rather than circular. His findings included three laws of planetary motion. These laws influenced Newton's later discoveries concerning gravity.

Sir Isaac Newton. Sir Isaac Newton, who worked at the end of the seventeenth and first part of the eighteenth centuries, was able to apply earlier scientific knowledge to discover laws of gravitation and motion. His discoveries were largely unrecognized until another English astronomer, Edmund Halley, consulted him about a problem. With Halley's financial aid, Newton published his laws in book form. Newton's laws are usually considered an outstanding contribution to modern scientific discovery. Newton also made discoveries concerning light and color, paving the way for the development of spectrum analysis.

Answer the following question.

1.72 What contributions to science have the following men made?

a. Roger Bacon ____

____

b. Leonardo da Vinci ____

____

____

c. Nicolaus Copernicus ____

____

d. Galileo ____

____

____

e. Johannes Kepler ____

____

____

f. Sir Isaac Newton ____

____

____

Complete this activity.

1.73 Do some research about one of the Renaissance figures you have studied. Find out more about his life and his contributions. Write a short paper, about one and a half or two pages, and turn it in to your teacher.

TEACHER CHECK ____________ initials ____________ date

Review the material in this section in preparation for the Self Test. The Self Test will check your mastery of this particular section. The items missed on this Self Test will indicate specific areas where restudy is needed for mastery.

SELF TEST 1

Answer true or false (each answer, 1 point).

1.01 __________ The Renaissance marked a drastic change from the darkness of the Middle Ages to the rebirth of knowledge.

1.02 __________ Wars tended to encourage the Renaissance.

1.03 __________ Towns sprang up as a result of the growth of trade encouraged by the crusades.

1.04 __________ The government of France was stable during the Hundred Years' War.

1.05 __________ The restrictions imposed upon Edward II by the barons led to a parliamentary type of government.

1.06 __________ The Wars of the Roses was won by the French.

1.07 __________ The Renaissance encouraged a more centralized form of government and a sounder economy in most Western European countries.

1.08 __________ The Tudor dynasty, established by Henry VII brought peace and prosperity to England.

1.09 __________ Italy was composed of five relatively wealthy states during the fourteenth and fifteenth centuries.

1.010 __________ A *duke* is the same thing as a *doge*.

Complete the following statements (each answer, 3 points).

1.011 The French general who led under Charles V was ______________________________.

1.012 The country famous for weaving woolen cloth was ______________________________.

1.013 The Hundred Years' War resulted in many battles being won by the

a. ______________________, but the b. ______________________ won the war.

1.014 One of the most powerful political families in Italy was the ______________________ family.

1.015 The gold coin used as a standard for Europe was the ______________________________.

1.016 The Wars of the Roses was between the a. ______________________________ and the

b. ______________________ over c. ______________________________.

1.017 Giotto was a famous Renaissance ______________________________.

1.018 The three greatest Renaissance painters were a. ______________________________,

b. ______________________, and c. ______________________________.

Match the following terms with the correct answer (each answer, 2 points).

1.019 _______ *The Prince*

1.020 _______ Christian humanism

1.021 _______ *Utopia*

1.022 _______ *Hamlet*

1.023 _______ *Don Quixote*

1.024 _______ *Decameron*

1.025 _______ "Mona Lisa"

1.026 _______ *The Praise of Folly*

a. an attempt to restore a purity to Christianity

b. an idealized society invented by Sir Thomas More

c. a play by Shakespeare

d. written by Boccaccioe.

e. painted by da Vinci

f. a book by Cervantes

g. a book by Machiavelli

h. written by Ben Jonson

i. written by Erasmus

Identify or explain these names or terms (each answer, 4 points).

1.027 heliocentric ____

____

1.028 oligarchy ____

____

1.029 Romanesque ____

____

1.030 mercenaries ____

____

1.031 Inquisition ____

____

1.032 Renaissance ____

____

HISTORY & GEOGRAPHY 1004

LIFEPAC TEST

NAME ________________________

DATE ________________________

SCORE ________________________

HISTORY & GEOGRAPHY 1004: LIFEPAC TEST

Write the letter for the best answer on each blank (each answer, 2 points).

1. Members of an important family of kings in England were called ______ .
a. Tudors b. Valois c. de Medicis d. Hapsburgs

2. A dispute between the English and the French over the French throne was known as the ______ .
a. Thirty Years War b. Hundred Years' War
c. *Wars of the Roses* d. *Pilgrimage of Grace*

3. French Calvinists were called ______ .
a. Lollards b. Jesuits c. Almohads d. Huguenots

4. The person most nearly meeting the description of the Renaissance ideal man was ______ .
a. John Calvin b. Michelangelo c. Henry VIII d. Leonardo da Vinci

5. A manual written by Machiavelli justifying any means used by a politician to achieve his goal was called ______ .
a. *Don Quixote* b. *The Prince* c. *The Praise of Folly* d. *Utopia*

6. A form of government in which only a privileged few have the power is called ______ .
a. a theocracy b. heliocentric c. an oligarchy d. a monarchy

7. A famous painting by Leonardo da Vinci was ______ .
a. "David" b. "The Last Judgment"
c. "The Last Supper" d. "The Prince"

8. A style of architecture using arches, flying buttresses, and stained glass is known, as ______ .
a. Gothic b. Romanesque c. Byzantine d. Baroque

9. The Protestant leader who made the first major translation of the Bible into English was ______ .
a. Martin Luther b. John Wycliffe c. John Huss d. John Calvin

10. The factor which was not a major consideration in the English Reformation was ______ .
a. a male heir to the throne b. the *Act of Supremacy*
c. The *Peace of Westphalia* d. religious dissatisfaction

Complete these statements (each blank, 3 points).

11. An important center for weaving woolen cloth was ______________________.

12. The conflict between the Yorkists and Lancastrians was known as ______________________.

13. A city which became the haven for over six thousand Protestants was ________________.

14. The Protestant leader who was captured and made a galley slave was ________________.

15. Four major areas in which change occurred during the Renaissance were a. ____________, b. ________________________, c. ___________________, and d. ______________________.

16. As a result of the Renaissance, strong monarchies rose out of these countries: a. ______________________, b. ______________________, and c. ______________________.

17. The pope was recognized as the authority on doctrine and the Catholic doctrines were reaffirmed by ____________________________________ which was convened by Charles V.

18. The three outstanding Renaissance painters were a. ________________________________, b. ______________________________, and c. _______________________________.

Match these items (each answer, 2 points).

19. _______ John of Gaunt
20. _______ Ignatius Loyola
21. _______ Charles V
22. _______ Mary Stuart
23. _______ Clement VII
24. _______ Thomas Cranmer
25. _______ Anglican
26. _______ Presbyterian
27. _______ Anabaptist
28. _______ Erasmus
29. _______ Henry of Navarre
30. _______ Gustavus II

a. founded the Jesuits
b. one of the popes
c. Church of England
d. church in Scotland governed by elders
e. a Christian humanist
f. first of the Bourbon kings
g. queen of England
h. sponsored John Wycliffe
i. reform movement rejecting infant baptism
j. queen of Scotland
k. Holy Roman Emperor
l. archbishop of Canterbury
m. Lutheran king of Sweden
n. queen of France

Complete the following lists (each answer, 2 points).

1.033 List four reasons leading to the Renaissance.

a. ______________________________

b. ______________________________

c. ______________________________

d. ______________________________

1.034 List four areas of change during the Renaissance.

a. ______________________________

b. ______________________________

c. ______________________________

d. ______________________________

84/105 **SCORE** __________ **TEACHER** __________ __________
initials date

2. THE REFORMATION

| Martin Luther's 95 Theses at All Saints' Church in Wittenberg

The Reformation refers to a sixteenth-and seventeenth-century religious movement which spread throughout Western Europe. This movement began with Protestant leaders, such as Martin Luther and John Calvin, in the first part of the sixteenth century.

The Reformation spread to England, where it had vast political implications. The English monarch Henry VIII gained control of the church, establishing the Anglican Church as the official religion. England became Protestant or Catholic, following the persuasion of each monarch. Reform movements were also taking place within the Catholic Church structure. Loyola and Pope Paul III were two very influential forces for church reform. The very strong feelings of each group ultimately resulted in a series of religious wars throughout Western Europe.

In this section you will learn more about the causes for the Reform Movement in Europe. Some of the philosophies and beliefs of the main Protestant leaders will be presented. Other developments in England led to the spread of Protestantism. You will discover the roles Henry VIII and his successors played in this religious movement. Not only a change from Catholicism to Protestantism, the Reformation also brought about changes within Catholicism.

This section will help you understand some of those internal religious changes. As a result of so much change within a little over a century, religious wars developed. You will learn more about the reasons for these struggles and more about the impact this period of history had in the shaping of the Western world.

Section Objectives

Review these objectives. When you have completed this section, you should be able to:

6. Trace the European Protestant Reformation.
7. Trace the development of the Reformation in England.
8. Trace the Catholic reform movement.
9. Describe the impact of the religious wars upon Western Europe.

Vocabulary

Study these words to enhance your learning success in this section.

Anglican **diet** **theocracy**

THE REFORMATION IN EUROPE

The Later Middle Ages produced a period of religious unrest in Western Europe. This dissatisfaction with the practices of the established church was intensified by such factors as the reaffirmation of the papal bull *Unam Sanctum*, which was an official statement issued by the pope stating that the pope was the head of both church and state.

Public dissatisfaction with some of the popes of the Renaissance grew. Money seemed to be the basis for granting favors and forgiveness. Catholic believers thought that a lowering of moral standards would result from the policy of "purchasing" forgiveness. Some of the high ranking clergy lived lives of luxury and indulgence, neglecting church duties.

Certain church abuses were also criticized: *Simony*, the buying or selling of church positions; *nepotism*, or granting positions as appointments to relatives; and the sale of *indulgences*, or the exchange of money for a penance, rather than an action.

Economic and political dissatisfaction also encouraged reform. The church holdings yielded little or no income to the monarchs. The monarchs felt deprived of the wealth produced by this property. Since these holdings were vast, many European monarchs decided to claim them.

The Reformation also provided the opportunity for the German princes to usurp much of the authority of the Holy Roman Emperor.

Some of the major figures working for reform included John Wycliffe, John Huss, Martin Luther, Ulrich Zwingli, Conrad Grebel, John Calvin, and John Knox.

John Wycliffe. A scholarly English theologian, John Wycliffe, was very concerned by the corruption in the established church. His writings vigorously denounced clerical abuses of the period and recommended drastic measures. He questioned papal authority, and he denied the right of a ruler to demand obedience on the claim that it was God's will. Wycliffe left Oxford and began to preach in London and to write for the royal family. He was sponsored by John of Gaunt and was thus protected from the church's anger. Although he was summoned twice for trial by the clergy, the royal family had him released.

Wycliffe became disenchanted because of the accusations of heresy. Then the papal schism of 1378 produced two rival popes when the French cardinals elected a French pope because they disliked the Italian pope. Each pope claimed office by divine right. This situation further disgusted Wycliffe, leading him to attack the office of the pope and the sacraments. He felt that the Bible was the only true measure for Christian conduct. His main contribution was that he and his followers made the first major translation of the Bible into English.

When Wycliffe became a revolutionist, he lost many supporters. Most of the people wanted changes but not an actual overthrow of the church. After John of Gaunt severed his relationship with Wycliffe, Wycliffe was banished from Oxford as a heretic.

Wycliffe's followers, known as Lollards, were persecuted as heretics. Although most of the Lollards denied their beliefs or escaped, many of these poor priests continued to spread Wycliffe's teachings without further persecution. When Sir John Oldcastle and thirty-six fellow Lollards were hanged as traitors, however, a renewed persecution of Lollards sent the movement underground. The teachings and writings of Wycliffe influenced reformers in other countries. Wycliffe was considered the first outstanding English reformer.

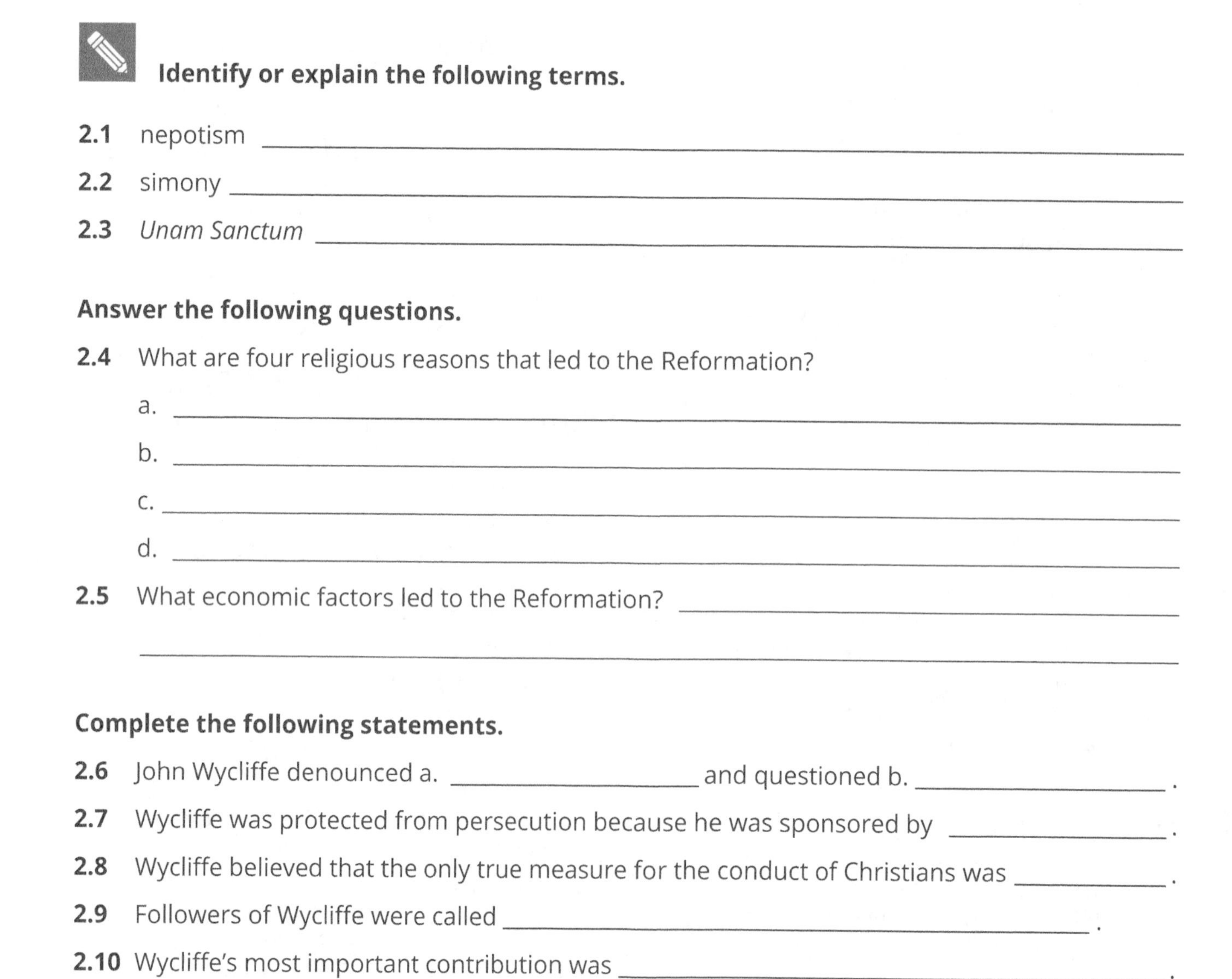

Identify or explain the following terms.

2.1 nepotism ______________________________

2.2 simony ______________________________

2.3 *Unam Sanctum* ______________________________

Answer the following questions.

2.4 What are four religious reasons that led to the Reformation?

a. ______________________________

b. ______________________________

c. ______________________________

d. ______________________________

2.5 What economic factors led to the Reformation? ______________________________

____

Complete the following statements.

2.6 John Wycliffe denounced a. ______________ and questioned b. ______________ .

2.7 Wycliffe was protected from persecution because he was sponsored by ______________ .

2.8 Wycliffe believed that the only true measure for the conduct of Christians was ______________ .

2.9 Followers of Wycliffe were called ______________ .

2.10 Wycliffe's most important contribution was ______________ .

John Huss. In Bohemia, Wycliffe's influence was reflected in the teachings of John Huss. Ordained a priest early in the fifteenth century, Huss attacked the church offices, not the sacraments. The papal schism was compounded in 1409 when a third pope denounced the other two and claimed papal authority. Huss was an opponent of the papacy because of this situation. When Huss was appointed rector of the University of Prague, the Germans resented his position and spread rumors of heresy. Huss was excommunicated and subsequently condemned to be burned at the stake. Huss' ideas were to influence Martin Luther.

After the death of Huss, his followers broke from the church and established the Unity of Brethren, or Moravian Church. This small localized organization could probably be called the first Protestant church.

Complete the following statements.

2.11 The man who spread Wycliffe's beliefs in Bohemia was ________________________________.

2.12 As a result of his teachings, and his position as rector of the University of Prague, Huss was

a. ________________________________ and b. ________________________________.

2.13 Huss' followers established the ____.

Martin Luther. Martin Luther's background influenced him to become an Augustine monk. Educated to believe that only God had the power to save man, Luther was not exposed to many humanistic ideas at the university. After nearly being killed by lightning, Luther became very aware of God and religion.

As a successful professor at the University of Wittenberg, Luther realized that faith in God would save man and that faith could be attained through reading the Bible. This idea was in conflict with the sale of indulgences and the Catholic belief that both faith and good works lead to salvation.

Disturbed by the lack of faith among monks he knew and the worldliness of the church officers, Luther protested against church teachings.

On October 31, 1517, Martin Luther nailed his Ninety-Five Theses to the door of the church at Wittenberg. These theses were proposals, or controversial beliefs, posted for public debate. Some of the ideas Luther expressed included the belief that the pope himself could not forgive sinners, but was only God's representative. The effects of Luther's action were far more widespread than he imagined. He had hoped to bring these issues to the attention of church and university leaders. Soon all of Germany was involved in debating these issues because the theses were translated into German and printed. Copies were sent into other countries as well. The people stopped buying indulgences, and the monks complained to Pope Leo. At that time the pope thought the issue would die down by itself.

By 1519, however, Luther was called before a papal council and asked to explain his beliefs. Luther admitted that his beliefs were similar to those of Huss, a condemned heretic. Luther attacked the mass, saying that all believers should partake of the Lord's Supper and that the service should not be restricted to the Latin language. Luther also disputed the number of sacraments, saying that Christ mentioned only two—the Lord's Supper and baptism. Luther claimed that marriage was not a sacrament, because it belonged to all people, not just to Christians. The sacraments included rites belonging exclusively to Christians.

The German state of Saxony, headed by Frederick the Wise, supported Luther. Emperor Charles V of the Holy Roman Empire was a devout Catholic. Charles V opposed Luther, whom he considered a heretic.

By 1520 the pope excommunicated Luther. Luther merely burned this decree, demonstrating that he was no longer a Catholic. He continued his teachings about the sacraments and salvation by faith alone. Because the pope could do no more to him, Pope Leo appealed to Emperor Charles V to use his powers. In 1521 Luther was tried at Worms. Appearing before the **Diet** of Worms, Luther refused to deny his beliefs.

Charles V decided against Luther, but Luther had already left. Frederick the Wise had instructed some men to hide Luther. Luther was sent to live at Wartburg castle, disguised as a knight with a beard. During this period Luther translated the Bible into German.

Some of Luther's followers rioted and caused domestic unrest. Fearing the movement would get out of hand, Luther went back to Wittenberg. He was not captured and punished, because Charles V was involved with a war. Luther set up his own church with the help of the Saxon rulers. His church and his followers became known as Protestants in 1529. The Protestants simplified the German church services, omitted the mass, and eliminated monastic orders from their church system. The Lutheran movement spread quickly. Peasants, thinking that Lutheranism would provide political solutions, revolted in an attempt to establish this religion and end feudalism. This violent revolt was put down easily. Luther lost the support of many peasants, because he did not back their movement. The Catholics took advantage of this split in Lutheranism to slow the Protestant movement.

| Martin Luther

The *Augsburg Confession* of 1530 set forth Lutheran doctrines. By the mid-sixteenth century Denmark, Norway, Sweden, and most of northern Germany had become Lutheran. Southern Germany remained Catholic.

Charles V attacked the Lutherans in 1546, the same year Luther died, and won for a time. However, France allied herself with the Protestants. A truce, the *Peace of Augsburg*, ended the war in 1555. This truce allowed each German prince to make the religious choice for his state. Any person disagreeing with the religion of his state had to conform or move. This religious difference combined with previous political differences prevented the rise of a strong national state of Germany.

Write the letter for the correct answer on each blank.

2.14 Martin Luther had been ______ .

a. a mathematics tutor
b. an Augustine monk
c. an experimental scientist
d. an archbishop

2.15 The Ninety-Five Theses were ______ .

a. a reading list
b. indulgences
c. sacraments
d. proposals

2.16 The idea *not* expressed by Luther is ______ .

a. The pope could not forgive sinners himself.
b. Marriage is a sacrament.
c. Faith in God would lead to salvation.
d. The service should not be conducted only in Latin.

2.17 Luther was supported by ______ .

a. Charles V
b. Frederick the Wise
c. the peasants
d. the Augsburg kings

2.18 Germany's political and religious differences ______ .

a. prevented its being a strong national state
b. led to an increased national spirit
c. resulted in the Hundred Years' War
d. led to the adoption of Catholicism

Ulrich Zwingli. A Swiss priest, Zwingli was deeply impressed by the fact that Martin Luther's ideas so closely paralleled his own. Encouraged by Luther's example, Zwingli preached in Zurich. Although Zwingli supported Luther's movement, the two men did not agree about all religious issues. Zwingli believed in a comprehensive reform of church practices and beliefs. Luther believed in the actual presence of Christ in Holy Communion, or the Lord's Supper. Zwingli believed that the bread and wine symbolized Christ's presence.

Zwingli supported a type of religion without saints, fasting, and celibate priests. Zurich was persuaded to adopt a **theocratic** form of government, which was initiated by other Swiss cities.

Luther was trying to negotiate with German Catholics at a time Zurich Protestants were trying vigorously to convert Catholics. In the resulting war Zwingli was killed.

Conrad Grebel. Another religious group in Zurich was known as the Swiss Brethren or Anabaptists. These Anabaptists, as they were called, believed in baptizing adults, because they could not find Scriptural confirmation of infant baptism. Rather than join other Protestant movements, the Anabaptists, led by Conrad Grebel, formed their own groups in Germany, in the Netherlands, as well as in Switzerland.

The Anabaptists also believed in separation of church and state. They believed in peace; the state believed in war. The state required the taking of oaths; Jesus forbade swearing. The Anabaptists were persecuted by Catholics and Protestants, and sometimes they were put to death for their beliefs. From this group of believers came Hutterites, the Mennonites, and indirectly the Baptists.

Answer these questions.

2.19 What were some of the religious beliefs expressed by Zwingli?

____

____

____

2.20 Where did Zwingli preach? ______________________________

2.21 How was Zwingli's approach in dealing with the German Catholics different from that of Luther?

____

____

2.22 What did the Anabaptists believe?

a. ____

b. ____

c. ____

d. ____

2.23 Who led the Anabaptist group? ______________________________

John Calvin. John Calvin, a French Protestant who had left France to avoid persecution, brought logic and organization to the ideas of Protestantism.

In 1536 Calvin published *Institutes of the Christian Religion*. In it are set forth his beliefs. This work is an outstanding example of literature of the Reformation. Calvin was chosen to lead the Geneva Protestants.

Calvin believed faith to be all-important. He felt that the Bible should be the only authority in religion; he denied the existing system of hierarchy in the Catholic Church. Calvin stood for a simplified form of church service and rejected the idea of the actual presence of Jesus Christ in the Lord's Supper. He believed in the separation of church and state. Calvin was convinced that God had chosen certain individuals to be saved—the elect—at the time of creation. He taught that man should lead a Christlike life to be united with Christ.

The Calvinistic form of church government is said to be *Presbyterian*; *presbyter* is a Greek word meaning *elder*. The governing group, called a session, consists of the elders or older men of the church and the minister. The sessions have representation in church councils, or *presbyteries*. The *synods*, or regional assemblies are formed by representatives from each presbytery. Calvinism encouraged a constitutional form of government, representation of the people, and separation of church and state.

Calvin was the head of a theocracy in Geneva. A strict believer, he prohibited such activities as dancing, gambling, and wearing colorful or ornamental apparel.

Geneva soon became a haven for those Protestants seeking escape from persecution. Some six thousand Protestants came from England, France, Italy, Scotland, and Spain. Calvin worked diligently to serve these refugees.

| John Calvin

Many of the Calvinists were extreme in their religious zeal. Some Protestants not believing in Calvinism were sent out of the country or punished for their heresy. Michel Servet, who denied Jesus' divinity and the existence of the Holy Spirit, was burned at the stake.

In the Netherlands, Calvinists formed the Dutch Reformed Church. Calvinism played an important role in the revolt against Spain.

John Knox. In Scotland, John Knox, a Calvinist, established the Presbyterian Church. Knox, a former Catholic priest, had been influenced by George Wisehart, a Protestant. Wisehart was burned as a heretic by a cardinal who was in turn assassinated by some Protestants. The French joined Mary, the Catholic princess of Scotland, against the band of Protestant rebels.

Although Knox was not one of the assassins, he was arrested with other Protestants and made a galley slave.

Released in 1549, Knox became a Protestant minister in England. When Mary Tudor restored Catholicism to England, Knox fled to Geneva. There he was influenced by Calvin and his beliefs.

After Queen Mary's death, Queen Elizabeth restored Protestantism, allowing the return of Knox to Scotland.

Answer true or false.

2.24 ____________ John Calvin was chosen to lead the Protestants in Geneva.

2.25 ____________ Calvin believed in the combination of church and state.

2.26 ____________ Calvin restricted many personal practices of Protestants, such as gambling and dancing.

2.27 ____________ Zurich soon became a haven for over six thousand Protestants.

2.28 ____________ Calvin preached the theory of the *elect*.

2.29 ____________ John Knox established the Presbyterian Church.

2.30 ____________ John Knox was a galley slave.

2.31 ____________ Mary Tudor restored Protestantism to England.

2.32 ____________ Knox returned to Scotland when Elizabeth became queen.

THE REFORMATION IN ENGLAND

Earlier criticisms of church problems by loyal Catholics occurred during the Renaissance. Colet, More, and Erasmus worked for internal church reforms. Their writing and questioning encouraged later reforms.

Although the early sixteenth-century English Church had some problems with heretics, no reform movement concerning church doctrine had yet begun. However, earlier antipapal feelings had been demonstrated. The concept of separation of church and state was encouraged by papal involvement in wars and politics, as well as by a new spirit of nationalism. Public opinion turned against the clergy as a result of common abuses and corruption among some members of the clergy.

Henry VIII. Hoping to use public opinion against the clergy to his advantage, Henry VIII used Parliament to attack papal power in hopes of forcing the pope to grant his wishes. Parliament, in 1529, restricted the power of papal dispensations. With the help of Thomas Cromwell, his chief advisor, Henry then made other accusations and demanded that he, as king, be declared the head of the English Church. With certain exceptions, the church tried to comply with Henry's demand. Parliament asked the king, as head of the church, to do away with certain church abuses. Henry had laws passed that gave him control of the clergy. No church laws could be passed without the king's approval. Henry passed an act restricting large sums usually paid to the pope by newly appointed archbishops and bishops. He offered to amend each if the pope would grant him an annulment.

Catherine of Aragon, Henry's wife, was Catholic. She had not been able to give him a male heir. Of her six children, only Princess Mary lived past infancy. Henry VIII wanted a male heir to continue his dynasty. He was also attracted to Anne Boleyn and was determined to marry her. Henry appealed to the pope for an annulment of his marriage. Pope Clement VII realized the religious problems posed by this action. The pope depended upon Emperor Charles V of the Holy Roman Empire, who was Catherine's nephew. The pope tried to postpone his decision. Henry grew tired of waiting for the pope's decision and decided to bypass papal authority. He set out to secure supreme power in England by having Thomas Cranmer appointed Archbishop of Canterbury. This action placed a king's representative as the head of England's highest ecclesiastical, or church, court. Appealing to the archbishop, Henry sought and received approval from Cranmer for his annulment. The annulment was granted on the basis of a supposed irregularity in the marriage. Henry married Anne Boleyn in 1533 and was promptly excommunicated by the pope.

Henry was disappointed in his hope for a son. Anne Boleyn had a daughter, Elizabeth. Henry VIII accused Anne of adultery, had her arrested, and beheaded. He then was married a third time to Jane Seymour, who died shortly after giving birth to a son, Edward, who would inherit the throne as Edward VI. A fourth marriage to Anne of Cleves, a political alliance, ended shortly by annulment. Catherine Howard, Henry's fifth wife, was also accused of adultery and beheaded. Only his sixth wife, Catherine Parr, escaped the fates of her predecessors. She outlived Henry.

In 1534 Henry VIII had Parliament pass the "Act of Supremacy," which proclaimed the king as the head of the Church of England, called the **Anglican** Church. This Anglican Church was to be separate from the mother church, although its doctrines—except for papal authority—remained the same. As head of the church, Henry executed Sir Thomas More who refused to accept Henry as head of the church. Others were punished in like manner.

In 1534 Henry secured his dynasty by having Parliament assure that the children of Anne Boleyn would become his heirs to the crown. This act was called the *Act of Succession*.

To gain public support, Henry closed the monasteries, distributing their lands to his supporters. Cromwell carried out the dissolving of the monasteries by claiming various instances of corruption. Much of the corruption reported by Cromwell may have been exaggerated. Monasteries were no longer essential to learning, nor were they able to provide adequate financial support to the people or to the state. In 1536 and 1539 the monasteries were completely dissolved by Parliament, making the king and his supporters wealthier and committing those recipients of church property to the Anglican Church structure.

In 1536 a group of peasants and some of the landed gentry joined in a rebellion called the *Pilgrimage of Grace*. These rebels demanded restoration of Catholicism and monasteries. They blamed Cromwell for the changes in church policy because they still believed in the king. The king sent royal representatives to discuss differences with the rebels. The royal representatives were outnumbered and had to grant the rebel's wishes. Some rebels attacked the king's men, breaking the agreement. The king refused to honor the agreement and had many rebels executed.

In 1537 Henry permitted an English translation of the Bible. Another translation, largely the work of William Tyndale, was authorized a few years later. Henry was unaware of Tyndale's part in this work; without knowing it, Henry had helped the Protestant cause. By translating the Bible from the Greek and Hebrew originals, Tyndale changed some of the meanings from the accepted Latin version used by the Catholic Church and gave his translation of the Bible a more Protestant slant. In 1539 Henry persuaded Parliament to pass the *Act of the Six Articles* which established the doctrine of the Anglican Church. Except for usurpation of papal authority, basically it supported Catholic beliefs. Henry disapproved of the practice of allowing the people to determine the meanings of the Scriptures, yet he allowed them access to the Bible in their own language. He persecuted both Catholics and Lutherans, sometimes violently, when they worked against or spoke against the Church of England.

Henry established the line of succession before his death. The crown was to pass first to Edward VI, then to Mary I, and finally to Elizabeth I.

Complete the following statements.

2.33 The Reformation in England was both a a. ______________________ and a b. ______________________ movement.

2.34 Henry VIII was first married to ______________________.

2.35 Henry wanted to divorce his first wife because he wanted to establish ______________.

2.36 Henry became head of the Church of England as a result of the ______________________ passed by Parliament in 1534.

2.37 The *Pilgrimage of Grace* was ______________________.

2.38 Tyndale translated the Bible from the original a. ______________________________ and b. ______________________________ into c. ______________________________.

2.39 The *Act of the Six Articles* established ______________________________.

2.40 Henry VIII persecuted both Catholics and Protestants if they spoke against ______________ ______________________________.

Edward VI. Only nine years old when he inherited the English crown in 1547, Edward VI was a sickly youngster. The council of regents was established by Henry VIII to help rule the kingdom until his son was of age. The earl of Hertford, Edward VI's uncle, dominated the council, was appointed lord protector, and was declared Duke of Somerset. As lord protector, Somerset convinced the young king to grant him the power to rule the kingdom.

Somerset was confronted with foreign problems. England was in debt because of the war with France. The French were unhappy with the English possession of Boulogne. An alliance between Scotland and France was prompted by Somerset's invasion of Scotland. The Scots and French agreed to the marriage of the infant queen of Scots, Mary Stuart, and the French heir to the throne, Francis.

Somerset passed legislation which encouraged the Protestant movement. Members of the clergy were permitted to marry. English was used in much of the church service. *The Book of Common Prayer*, a new prayer book prepared by Archbishop Cranmer, was required under the First Act of Uniformity in 1549.

Somerset also continued the confiscation of religious properties, a practice which had been started by Henry VIII. Although Henry had also begun destroying certain religious relics, Protestants began demolishing cathedrals and other symbols of Catholicism under Somerset. Religious feelings were strong.

England suffered financial problems during this period of religious turmoil. Unemployment, displaced populations, rising prices, and increased crime occurred. One reason for these economic problems was that the increased flow of gold and silver from the new world caused the depreciation of the value of gold and the increase of prices for food and other necessities. Another reason was the debasement of coins, started by Henry VIII. He had used more alloy and less gold for each coin. Somerset could not relieve the financial crisis, although he tried. A third factor was the system of enclosures, the practice of enclosing large tracts of land for agriculture, parks, or pasture. This capitalistic use of lands caused a rise in rents.

In 1548 Somerset ordered a stop to enclosure to help the common people; however, he was not supported by others of the ruling class. The frustrated peasants revolted in 1549. Around sixteen thousand peasants, led by Robert Kett destroyed barriers around these enclosures. The rebels looted but did not kill. Somerset attempted to deal peaceably with the rebels but had to resort to military tactics. As a result of this rebellion, Somerset lost the support of the council.

The earl of Warwick deposed Somerset and appointed himself Duke of Northumberland. Northumberland then established a reactionary policy. Enclosures were again restored. The peasants had no rights. Northumberland gave up Boulogne to France for half of the amount France had offered. He officially acknowledged the Scottish-French alliance by the proposed marriage between Mary Stuart and Francis. He also gave up all English territory in Scotland.

Northumberland's religious policies were more extreme than those of Somerset. More rigid rules were laid down for Anglican services.

Those people who did not adhere to these rules were punished.

In 1552 the Second Act of Uniformity was passed. In 1553 the council issued forty-two articles stating Anglican doctrine. Included in these articles were the denial of five of the seven sacraments, the affirmation of salvation through faith, and the denial of the actual presence of Christ in the "Holy Eucharist," or the "Lord's Supper."

Edward VI was afflicted with tuberculosis and his health was quickly failing. Northumberland wanted to claim the throne. Henry VIII had established the line of succession after Edward to pass to Mary Tudor and then to Elizabeth. Because Mary was a devout Catholic she would not be at all sympathetic to the Protestant Northumberland who feared that he would lose his life at Mary's succession to the throne. Northumberland began to plot against her succession.

Since he had been able to appoint his men to the council, Northumberland virtually controlled the government. He was also successful in persuading the dying young Edward VI to bequeath the crown to a Protestant. Lady Jane Grey and her male descendants were made heirs to the throne.

Lady Jane Grey became Northumberland's daughter-in-law when she married his son, Guildford Dudley. Upon Edward's death in 1553, Lady Jane Grey was crowned queen.

Mary refused to have her right to the throne usurped. She called together an army of supporters which far exceeded Northumberland's troops. He returned to London to find his cause defeated. Mary held most of the support and was crowned queen. Lady Jane was deposed and Northumberland was imprisoned and executed.

Match the following items. You may use an answer more than once.

2.41 _______ Robert Kett

2.42 _______ Guildford Dudley

2.43 _______ Archbishop Cranmer

2.44 _______ Lady Jane Grey

2.45 _______ Henry VIII

2.46 _______ Northumberland

2.47 _______ Somerset

a. prepared a new prayer book

b. became lord protector

c. used more alloy, less gold to debase coins

d. ordered a stop to enclosure

e. led rebels against enclosures

f. deposed Somerset

g. was crowned queen upon Edward's death

h. Northumberland's son and Lady Jane Grey's husband

Complete the following statements.

2.48 Edward VI was ________________ years old when he became king.

2.49 Henry VIII had appointed a ____________________ to help his son rule if he were not of age when he inherited the throne.

2.50 Edward's uncle, ____________________________________, was appointed lord protector.

2.51 List three factors that caused economic problems in England:

a. ____

____,

b. ____, and

c. ____.

2.52 Northumberland began to plot against the succession to the throne of ________________.

2.53 When Edward died in 1553, ____________________________________ was crowned queen.

Mary I. Mary's childhood had been desperately unhappy. Her mother had been divorced by her father. Then Mary was separated from her mother and persecuted in various ways for being devoutly Catholic in times of Protestant domination. Naturally, Mary harbored some bitterness. Since her early solace had been her religion, Mary was convinced she should restore Catholicism to England as the state religion.

After her succession to the throne, Mary immediately restored the Catholic religion and released many church officers who had been imprisoned. She appointed Bishop Gardiner as Lord Chancellor and as royal advisor. Parliament repealed most of the Protestant legislation except the supremacy and disallowed punishment of nonpracticing Catholics.

Mary's major allies during Edward's rule had been the Spanish ambassadors to England. In an effort to further Catholicism, Mary insisted on arranging a marriage with Philip of Spain, who was the son of Charles V. Bishop Gardiner tried to warn her that her subjects would resent foreign intervention by Philip. Mary continued pursuing her plans for marriage.

The announcement of Mary's wedding plans resulted in rebellion. Mary's troops defeated the rebels in London. Although Lady Jane Grey was not involved in the plot to overthrow Mary, she, her husband, and several others were executed. Princess Elizabeth, however, was released because she was popular and there was no evidence of her involvement in the rebellion.

Mary was able to persuade Parliament to restore papal authority. The previously confiscated lands, however, were not restored. She then began active persecution of Protestant heretics. Instead of weakening the Protestant movement, the martyrs strengthened Protestant feelings. Almost three hundred Protestants were burned at the stake. Not only Protestants, but many loyal Catholics were repulsed by Mary's persecutions. She became known as "Bloody Mary."

Mary's unpopularity grew. When she decided to help her husband in the Spanish war with France, the pope protested. With Mary's death, Catholicism as the state religion of England died.

Answer true or false.

2.54 ____________ Mary Tudor deposed Lady Jane Grey.

2.55 ____________ Mary was bitter because she had suffered religious persecution and separation from her mother.

2.56 ____________ Mary was a devout Catholic.

2.57 ____________ Mary married Philip of France.

2.58 ____________ Mary turned against the Catholics and burned almost three hundred of them at the stake.

2.59 ____________ Mary was the daughter of Anne Boleyn.

Elizabeth I. Elizabeth, the daughter of Anne Boleyn, succeeded Mary as queen of England in 1558. Although her father, Henry VIII, had been popular, this popularity had died out since his reign. With the throne, Elizabeth inherited the threat of a civil war and several other problems. Foreign relations were tangled. England was at odds with French influence in Scotland as well as embroiled with the Spanish.

Elizabeth was a well-qualified person to meet the challenges of her reign. She had inherited the Tudor traits of shrewdness and the ability to deal efficiently with people. She had been educated and had acquired a great deal of experience with people and problems. Elizabeth also had a great deal of self-confidence, having survived all the plots against her. A very complex woman, Elizabeth combined the traits of a politician with those of a petulant, willful child.

In 1559 Parliament indicated its willingness to revert back to Protestantism. The Act of Supremacy replaced Mary's Catholic legislation with most of the Protestant legislation passed earlier by Henry VIII. The Act of Uniformity dealt with the Anglican Church doctrine. Later additions to the law included a modified form of the forty-two articles of Edward VI's reign.

| Elizabeth I

Philip II of Spain proposed marriage to Elizabeth I to prevent England's becoming entirely Protestant and to prevent an English-French alliance. Although her rejection might alienate Spain in a French-English conflict or cause Spain and France to ally themselves against England, Elizabeth I refused his marriage offer.

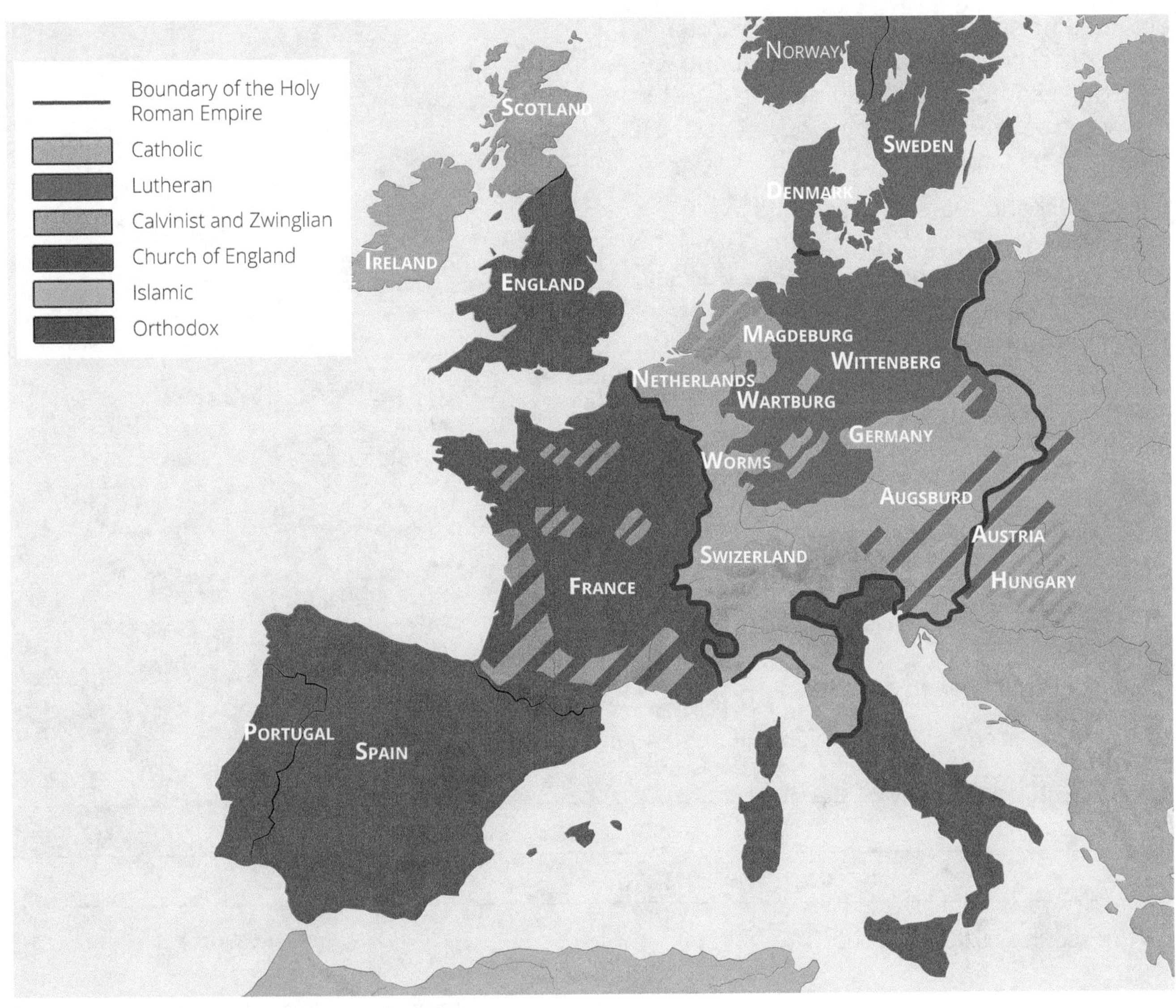

| Religions of Western Europe in 1570

Mary Stuart, queen of Scotland, claimed the English throne on the grounds that Henry VIII had not been married to Elizabeth's mother in the eyes of the Roman Catholic Church. Mary claimed her right through Henry's sister Margaret. Mary by this time had married Francis.

In 1559 Francis became king of France. Spain and France had just settled their differences by treaty. France was free to help Mary claim the English throne. Fortunately for Elizabeth, John Knox began his Reformation movement in Scotland at this time, creating a split in Scottish sentiment. The Scots rebelled against their French government, which was Catholic. Queen Elizabeth agreed to help free Scotland from French occupation. Since the French king was having domestic problems with religious changes, he could not aid his wife Mary Stuart. Mary agreed to the withdrawal of most French troops from Scotland. Papal power was replaced with Protestantism by the Scottish parliament.

Mary, queen of Scots, was widowed in 1560. In 1565 she married Lord Darnley, an English Catholic of royal lineage. By this marriage, Mary hoped to strengthen her claim to the throne and to win Catholic support. Darnley, however, provided no support for Mary's claim. After a series of scandals, Mary and her husband were forced to go into exile for a time. She gave birth to a son who would become King James VI of Scotland and James I of England.

Mary's husband, Darnley, was killed in an explosion. When only a few months later Mary married the man suspected of killing Darnley, she was forced to abdicate. She finally fled to England, where she continued to plot against Queen Elizabeth, who was her cousin. Elizabeth had Mary imprisoned for plotting against her. Mary was beheaded in 1587 for her involvement in a plot against Elizabeth's life.

Complete each activity.

2.60 Explain some of the problems in England in 1558, when Elizabeth inherited the throne.

____

____

____

2.61 Describe Elizabeth's characteristics.

____

____

____

Answer true or false.

2.62 ______________ Elizabeth restored Protestantism to England.

2.63 ______________ The *Act of Supremacy* established Anglican Church doctrine.

2.64 ______________ Elizabeth's marriage to Philip II of Spain caused problems.

2.65 ______________ Mary Stuart, queen of Scotland, claimed that the English throne was rightfully hers.

Write the letter for the correct answer on each blank.

2.66 Mary Stuart was not ______ .

a. a daughter of Henry VIII
b. a wife to Francis of France
c. a contender for the English throne
d. a Catholic

2.67 Philip II of Spain proposed marriage to Elizabeth because he wanted ______ .

a. to help Mary claim the English throne
b. to alienate Spain in a French-English conflict
c. to prevent England from becoming entirely Protestant
d. to gain popularity in Spain

2.68 The factor preventing France from helping Mary claim the throne was ______ .

a. her marriage to Philip
b. Elizabeth's decision to help Scotland
c. the friendship between Mary and Elizabeth
d. the French-English alliance of 1559

2.69 Mary hoped to strengthen her claim to the throne by ______ .

a. becoming Protestant
b. withdrawing her troops from France
c. tolerating John Knox
d. marrying Lord Darnley

Complete this activity.

2.70 Do some outside reading about Elizabethan England. Take notes on this information. Set up a panel of several of your classmates to discuss your findings or present the information as a class report—oral or written.

TEACHER CHECK ______ initials ______ date

REFORMATION WITHIN THE CATHOLIC CHURCH

The counter-Reformation, or Catholic Reformation, had its beginnings before Luther's Ninety-Five Theses. As a result of Protestant pressures, the need for church reform was intensified.

Three major areas of church reform include the influence of Ximénez in Spain; the founding of the Jesuit Society of Ignatius Loyola, also in Spain; and the decisions of the Council of Trent.

Ximénez. The major Spanish figure for church reform was the Franciscan Cardinal Ximénez. His first public office was that of Queen Isabella's confessor. She was impressed with his knowledge and wisdom in religious and political matters. Ximénez gradually assumed positions of responsibility until he was appointed a cardinal and the Chancellor of the state.

Despite his high offices, Ximénez chose to live a simple life. Wearing simple robes and going barefoot, Ximénez tried to reform the Spanish Friars. He even convinced Queen Isabella and several church officials that his way was God's way.

By the time of Ximénez, printing had been discovered. In his desire to make the Bible more widely available, Ximénez was responsible for the first printed edition of the whole Bible in the original languages—Old Testament Hebrew and New Testament Greek.

His Bible was called *Complutensian Polyglot*; the first word refers to the town in which it was printed and the second word means more than one language.

After Queen Isabella died, Ximénez worked with Ferdinand and Philip of Burgundy, Ferdinand's son-in-law who succeeded to the throne of Castile. Philip died in 1506, leaving Ximénez in control of Castile for a year.

Ximénez filled his office as cardinal until Ferdinand's death in 1516, when young Charles V succeeded to the throne and Ximénez served as his regent. Ximénez died in 1517.

Jesuit society. Spain was a center for Catholicism in the sixteenth century. It was also the strongest European military power of this time. Out of this Catholic stronghold grew a new religious order, *The Society of Jesus*. The founder of this order was Ignatius of Loyola.

Loyola, a young soldier, had been seriously wounded in 1522. He had experienced a religious conversion, choosing to support Catholicism. He studied theology in Paris and became a priest. Deciding to set up a new order in which to practice his ideas and beliefs, Loyola and nine others, including Francis Xavier, established the "Company of Jesus" in 1534. By 1540, Pope Paul III approved the order, now called "The Society of Jesus." The Jesuits, as members of this order were called, took vows of chastity, poverty, and obedience, yet did not lead cloistered lives. The Jesuits were organized in military fashion. Each member obeyed his superior. Only members of the upper class with intelligence, education, physical fitness, and strong character could be eligible for membership. The Jesuits spread Catholicism among infidels, Protestants, and Catholics who had strayed from basic Catholic beliefs. The influence of the Jesuits spread throughout Europe. Jesuits appeared in royal courts and in other positions of political influence.

The Council of Trent. The popes took the lead in church reform during the 16th century. The Council of Trent paved the way. Convened in 1545 by Charles V to deal with the Lutheran Protestants, for eighteen years, the council met whenever the need arose. Although it failed to provide an answer for all of the protesting, the council decreed certain reforms in the church. It encouraged more discipline among the members of the clergy, and provided for the removal of church abuses. Made up of European church leaders, it recognized the Pope's authority on doctrine. The church's doctrines of the seven sacraments, indulgences, purgatory, and the saints were reaffirmed by the council.

It provided for the education of the clergy and its candidates in all matters of the priesthood.

Other papal methods. The pope attempted to restrict the spread of Protestantism by enforcing Catholic principles. Three methods used were the concordats, the Index, and the Inquisition. Concordats were made with the various Catholic rulers of Europe. The monarchs were accorded a little more freedom from papal controls in return for supporting Catholicism in their respective countries. These concordats helped to prevent southern Europe from supporting Protestantism.

Pope Paul IV drew up the Index which was a list of books that Catholics were forbidden to read. The College of Cardinals used the Index so effectively that some books listed are known only by the title on the list.

A special church court called the Inquisition was established in the thirteenth century to deal with heretics. The Inquisition was used in later centuries as a method for identifying, judging, and punishing anyone, Catholic or Protestant, who was suspected of being troublesome to the church. The Spanish Inquisition became notorious because it employed such tactics as spying, torture, and execution. Because of the Inquisition, heresy was suppressed in Spain and Italy.

| The Council of Trent

Complete the following statements.

2.71 Cardinal Ximénez first held office as ______________________________.

2.72 Ximénez grew more responsible in politics, serving as a. ______________________________, b. ______________________________, and finally as c. ______________________________ for Charles V.

2.73 Ximénez is remembered as being responsible for the first ______________________________ ______________________________ ______________________________.

2.74 The founder of *"The Society of Jesus"* was ______________________________.

2.75 Jesuits took vows of a. ______________, b. ______________, and c. ______________.

2.76 The Jesuits were organized in ______________ fashion.

Complete these activities.

2.77 All Jesuits had to be

a. ____,

b. ____,

c. ____, and

d. ____.

2.78 List three decrees of the Council of Trent.

a. ____

b. ____

c. ____

2.79 List three methods the pope used to enforce Catholic principles.

a. ____

b. ____

c. ____

WARS OF RELIGION

Feelings between Catholics and Protestants grew bitter. Each side was convinced that adherence to its beliefs was the only way to salvation. Each group was convinced the other's beliefs were heresy. Conflicts in religion knew no boundaries. Civil wars erupted, resulting in conflicts between friends and even between family members.

War In France. France was torn by religious differences that resulted in the development of three groups of thought. One group consisted of the Huguenots, or French Calvinists. Another group included Catholics who wanted Catholicism as the only national religion. A third group, the *Politiques*, were Catholics who were more interested in politics than in religion.

Although the Huguenots were allowed to practice without persecution after 1560, France remained officially Catholic. Attempting to unite France, the Queen Mother Catherine arranged a marriage between her Catholic daughter and the leader of the French Huguenots, King Henry of Navarre. However, a Huguenot leader who was a guest of the royal wedding was killed. To prevent Protestant retaliation, Catherine decided to wipe out Protestantism by a massive attack on the Protestants on Saint Bartholomew's day. *The Massacre of Saint Bartholomew,* as it was called, resulted in the deaths of ten thousand Parisian Protestants.

After several years of bloodshed, Henry of Navarre became King Henry IV of France in 1589. He began the line of kings known as the Bourbon kings. Although he had been a Huguenot, Henry IV became Catholic to ease religious tensions. In 1598, he proclaimed the *Edict of Nantes*, which gave Protestants more freedom. They could hold some government offices, hold public worship services in certain cities, and worship privately without persecution. This edict ended the series of religious wars in France.

War in the Netherlands. The Netherlands of the sixteenth century was made up of seventeen provinces including the area now known as Belgium. The people of the Netherlands were divided by language and religion. The Dutch-speaking people of the northern provinces became Calvinistic, but the Flemish-speaking and French-speaking people of the southern provinces remained Catholic.

When Philip II of Spain took over the Netherlands in 1555, he brought Catholicism, Spanish control, and taxation. The people rebelled, forming mobs and spreading destruction among that country's Catholic churches. A special court was set up to deal with these Protestant rebels. Many Protestants were put to death; others fled, sacrificing their personal property for their lives. These exiled Protestants continued their revolutionary activities. Finally, Philip brought about a compromise, winning the Catholics of Flanders over to his side. After the English defeated the fleet of Spanish warships known as the *Spanish Armada* in 1588, Spain lost the opportunity to control the complete area.

War in Germany. Another religious struggle developed in Germany. The Thirty Years War grew out of religious and political problems. Religious intolerance, combined with commercial rivalry, resulted in uneasy alliances between former enemies to oppose an even greater threat—the Hapsburgs.

In Bohemia, Protestant nobles rebelled against the threat of a Catholic king, starting a power struggle against the Holy Roman Emperor. The Emperor's army invaded Germany. In 1629 Emperor Ferdinand signed the *Edict of Restitution*, restoring Catholic lands and restricting the religious and political rights of Protestants, except for Lutherans. Gustavus II of Sweden, a Lutheran, led an attack against the feared Hapsburg Catholics in Germany. Protestants joined together to drive out the German Hapsburgs.

By 1635, the Hapsburg rulers of Spain and of the Holy Roman Empire united against Protestant Germany, Holland, France, and Sweden. After thirteen more years of war, a truce was finally agreed upon in 1648. *The Peace of Westphalia*, as the agreements were called, contained many details.

These treaties set up boundaries and regulations for over three hundred states of Germany. Religious provisions were made to insure that Calvinists and Lutherans had the same rights and that the religion of each state would be determined by the head of that state.

These provisions brought an end to religious turmoil. The power of the Hapsburgs had been curtailed; Germany was now composed of many monarchies instead of individual city-states. Germany was still, however, a long way from becoming a national power.

The treaties of Westphalia also recognized the northern Protestant section of the Netherlands as the independent country of Holland. The Catholic Spanish Netherlands later became Belgium.

Answer true or false.

2.80 ____________ France became Protestant officially in 1560.

2.81 ____________ A marriage was arranged between the Catholic princess of France and the Protestant king of Navarre.

2.82 ____________ King Henry IV of France became the first of the Bourbon kings.

2.83 ____________ *The Edict of Nantes* gave Protestants more freedom.

2.84 ____________ The series of French wars ended in 1558.

2.85 ____________ The Netherlands was a united country by the sixteenth century.

Write the letter for the correct answer on each blank.

2.86 A Huguenot leader was killed ______ .

a. in church
b. at a royal wedding
c. at a funeral
d. in his own home

2.87 The *Massacre of Saint Bartholomew* ______ .

a. was the idea of Catherine, the Queen Mother
b. was the idea of Henry Navarre
c. resulted in about five hundred deaths
d. occurred in Aragon

2.88 The people of the northern part of the Netherlands were ______ .

a. Dutch- speaking and Catholic
b. Flemish- or French- speaking and Catholic
c. Dutch- speaking and Calvinistic
d. Flemish- or French- speaking and Calvinistic

2.89 The people of the southern provinces of the Netherlands were ______ .

a. Dutch- speaking and Catholic
b. Flemish- or French- speaking and Catholic
c. Dutch- speaking and Calvinistic
d. Flemish- or French- speaking and Calvinistic

2.90 In 1555 the Netherlands were taken over by ______ .

a. France
b. England
c. Flanders
d. Spain

Complete this list.

2.91 List three religious groups in France.

a. ______________________________

b. ______________________________

c. ______________________________

Explain or identify these terms or words.

2.92 Huguenots - ______________________________

2.93 *Politiques* - ______________________________

2.94 *The Spanish Armada* - ______________________________

2.95 Thirty Years War - ______________________________

____

2.96 *Edict of Restitution* - ______________________________

____

2.97 Gustavus II - ______________________________

____

2.98 Peace of Westphalia - ______________________________

____

____

____

Before taking this last Self Test, you may want to do one or more of these self checks.

1. ________ Read the objectives. Determine if you can do them.

2. ________ Restudy the material related to any objectives that you cannot do.

3. ________ Use the **SQ3R** study procedure to review the material.

a. **S**can the sections.

b. **Q**uestion yourself again (review the questions you wrote initially).

c. **R**ead to answer your questions.

d. **R**ecite the answers to yourself.

e. **R**eview areas you didn't understand.

4. ________ Review all vocabulary, activities, and Self Tests, writing a correct answer for each wrong answer.

SELF TEST 2

Answer true or false (each answer, 1 point).

2.01 __________ One of the most powerful families in Italy during the Renaissance was the Hapsburg family.

2.02 __________ The *Wars of the Roses* was a dispute over the English throne by the Lancasters and the Yorks.

2.03 __________ *Don Quixote* was a famous painting by da Vinci.

2.04 __________ The Hundred Years War was fought mainly in England.

2.05 __________ The Thirty Years' War was brought to an end by the *Peace of Westphalia*.

2.06 __________ Queen Elizabeth I was a very capable, well-qualified monarch who led England to a period of greatness.

2.07 __________ The *Peace of Westphalia* established the rights of Protestants and allowed each German head of state to determine the state religion.

2.08 __________ Ximénez, an outstanding force for reform in religion and politics, was a Spaniard.

2.09 __________ Henry VIII was nine-years-old when he became king.

2.010 __________ Tyndale translated the Bible into Greek and Latin.

2.011 __________ Lady Jane Grey was crowned queen of England for a short period after Edward's death.

2.012 __________ The reformation in England was strictly religious.

Complete the following sentences (each answer, 3 points).

2.013 Four areas of change during the Renaissance were in the areas of a. ____________________ , b. ____________________ , c. ____________________ , and d. ____________________ .

2.014 The French general who brought organization and discipline to the French army was ____ .

2.015 The Tudor dynasty was established by a. ____________________ of b. ____________________ .

2.016 The heliocentric theory was devised by ____ .

2.017 Three other Renaissance scientists who made advances in astronomy include a. ______________________________ , b. ______________________________ , and c. ______________________________ .

2.018 The doctrine of the *elect* was taught by ________________________.

2.019 Members of a group of Protestants believing in peace, separation of church and state, and adult baptism were called ________________________.

2.020 Martin Luther nailed his ______________, or proposals, to the door of a German church.

2.021 The practice of granting favors or positions to one's own relatives is called ____________.

2.022 The followers of Wycliffe were called ________________________.

2.023 The Swedish Lutheran leader ________________________ led a movement to drive the Hapsburgs from Germany.

Match these Items (each answer, 2 points).

2.024 _______ mercenaries

2.025 _______ Calais

2.026 _______ *doge*

2.027 _______ oligarchy

2.028 _______ Renaissance

2.029 _______ Almohads

2.030 _______ *Politiques*

2.031 _______ hierarchy

2.032 _______ Huguenots

2.033 _______ Jesuits

2.034 _______ Inquisition

2.035 _______ Index

a. a battle which resulted in the defeat of French forces

b. a period of gradual change or transition

c. structure of officials in the Catholic Church

d. paid professional soldiers

e. a Muslim power which came from Africa

f. an Italian duke

g. a form of government by a privileged few

h. the Spanish fleet of warships

i. French Catholics primarily interested in government

j. a church court

k. founded by Ignatius Loyola

l. a list of books forbidden to Catholics

m. French Calvinists

n. an act dissolving the monasteries

Write the letter for the correct answer on each blank (each answer, 2 points).

2.036 The Catholic group established by Loyola in Spain was called the ____________________ .

a. Inquisition   b. *Nantes Edict*   c. Huguenots   d. Jesuits

2.037 The method *not* used by the pope to enforce Catholic principles was the ______________ .

a. Concordats   b. Inquisition   c. Lollards   d. Index

2.038 The man who spread Wycliffe's beliefs in Bohemia was ________________________ .

a. John of Gaunt   b. John Huss   c. John Calvin   d. John Knox

2.039 The city which became a haven for over six thousand Protestants was ______________ .

a. Zurich   b. Geneva   c. Milan   d. Wittenberg

Complete these activities (each answer, 5 points).

2.040 Describe the nature of the Protestant Reformation in England.

____

____

____

____

____

2.041 Explain the contributions or beliefs of several Protestant leaders.

____

____

____

____

____

84/105 **SCORE** ____________ **TEACHER** ____________ ____________

initials   date

Before taking the LIFEPAC Test, you may want to do one or more of these self checks.

1. ________ Read the objectives. Check to see if you can do them.
2. ________ Restudy the material related to any objectives that you cannot do.
3. ________ Use the SQ3R study procedure to review the material.
4. ________ Review activities, Self Tests, and LIFEPAC vocabulary words.
5. ________ Restudy areas of weakness indicated by the last Self Test.

GLOSSARY

Anglican .... Church of England.

bourgeoisie .... A person of the middle class. Originally a citizen or freeman of a French city.

Christian humanism .... A study of the humanities from a Christian point of view.

diet .... A formal assembly in the Holy Roman Empire to discuss and act upon public or state affairs.

heliocentric .... Having the sun as a center.

humanities .... Cultural studies, as opposed to the sciences, including language and literature (especially Latin and Greek), philosophy, and art.

Moors .... A member of a Muslim people of mixed Arab and Berber stock coming from northwestern Africa. The Moors invaded Spain and occupied it for 700 years.

Neoplatonism .... A philosophical and religious system composed of the writings of Plato and the elements of Christianity.

poet laureate .... A court poet.

theocracy .... A government in which God, or a god, is recognized as the supreme civil ruler and in which religious authorities rule the state as God's or a god's representatives.